P9-BYH-025

Has History Any Meaning?

BY THE SAME AUTHOR

Carl Becker
Hegel's Philosophy of History
The Problem of Burke's Political Philosophy

Has History Any Meaning?

A CRITIQUE OF POPPER'S PHILOSOPHY OF HISTORY

Burleigh Taylor Wilkins

CORNELL UNIVERSITY PRESS
ITHACA, NEW YORK

Copyright © 1978 by Cornell University

All rights reserved. Except for brief quotations in a review, this book, or parts thereof, must not be reproduced in any form without permission in writing from the publisher. For information address Cornell University Press, 124 Roberts Place, Ithaca, New York 14850.

First published 1978 by Cornell University Press.

Printed in the United States of America

Library of Congress Cataloging in Publication Data
(For library cataloging purposes only)

Wilkins, Burleigh Taylor.
Has history any meaning?

Includes index.
1. History—Philosophy. 2. Popper, Karl Raimund, Sir, 1902–
I. Title.
D16.8.W597 901 78-58054
ISBN 0-8014-1187-4

901
W684h

193489

To Brita Taylor Wilkins

Contents

Preface

I am indebted to the University of California for a Regents Faculty Fellowship, which helped me to complete this book; to the students in my courses in the philosophy of history and social science, political philosophy, and the philosophy of Karl Popper for some stimulating discussions—I have in mind especially Clifton B. Perry, Gary E. Jones, Kathleen Wilson, Fred Young, and Carolyn S. Boland; to my daughter Brita Taylor and to Joel Feinberg for their encouragement and moral support; to Joseph Agassi, who read the manuscript for Cornell University Press and made several useful suggestions; and to Kay Scheuer and James Twiggs of Cornell University Press for their excellent editorial assistance.

BURLEIGH TAYLOR WILKINS

Santa Barbara, California

Introduction

"Has History Any Meaning?" is the title of the last chapter of Karl Popper's *Open Society and Its Enemies,* a chapter which contains the essential features of Popper's philosophy of history. Since in writing this critique I have closely followed the arguments and organization of that chapter, I have chosen to adopt its title. But while my study is structured around the final chapter and Popper's Addenda to that book, it is in no sense restricted to them, as I frequently examine other works by Popper where doing so will help to clarify or evaluate an argument or point he has made in *The Open Society and Its Enemies.*

I consider Popper's reflections on historical explanation and historical interpretation, specifically his claim that historians use general laws in their explanations of historical phenomena but that these laws are usually trivial and that historians frequently resort to interpretations which are circular in nature. I pay particular attention to Popper's claim that, while such interpretations are not testable or falsifiable, there can nevertheless be rational grounds for preferring one historical interpretation over another. Perplexed by Popper's claim that "history" in the sense in which most people speak of it does not exist and that, therefore, history has no meaning, I turn to his discussion of wholes and trends in *The Poverty of His-*

toricism as a way of understanding and evaluating this claim. Finally I examine Popper's moral philosophy as it relates to his argument that while history has no meaning we can give it meaning, and I do this with special reference to the "dualism of facts and standards" which Popper develops in the Addenda to *The Open Society and Its Enemies.*

This book is not a historical study of the development of Popper's philosophy, but I do argue that his moral philosophy and his philosophy of history are in important respects recognizably Kantian. I do not discuss here the question whether Popper's own historical studies of Plato, Hegel, and Marx in *The Open Society and Its Enemies* are accurate; rather I regard these studies as the occasion or springboard from which Popper sets forth an original philosophy of history that deserves study and evaluation independently of the question of how well his historical scholarship endures. For reasons that will become clear in the text I do believe that historicism is a recognizable trend or aspect of contemporary philosophy, and I consider the validity of Popper's arguments against what he calls anti-naturalistic historicism and pro-naturalistic historicism. A future A. O. Lovejoy may someday distinguish thirteen varieties of historicism (as Lovejoy once distinguished thirteen varieties of pragmatism), but for present purposes it may prove useful to consider historicism in a somewhat more general way but with special reference to the questions of whether a predictive science of society is possible and whether the moral meaning or significance of history can be read off or inferred from the facts of history.

Karl Popper's *Logic of Scientific Discovery* is generally regarded as one of the most important works ever written in the philosophy of science, and his *Open Society and Its Enemies* is widely considered to be a classic, although a controversial one, in political philosophy. I regard Popper as being of equal importance as a philosopher of history, and among other things I try to show how his philosophy of science and his political philosophy affect the content of his philosophy of history. Without attempting even a sketch of contemporary philosophy of history, I shall briefly try to justify my claim concerning Popper's importance in this area to readers who may still think of him only or chiefly as a critic of Hegel and Marx or as a precursor of Carl G. Hempel. I believe that (if we ignore the question of political influence) Popper is as important to contemporary philosophy of history as Hegel was to that of the nineteenth century and for much the same reason: just as nineteenth-century philosophy of history was mainly an extended commentary on Hegel, so contemporary philosophy of history is largely an extended commentary on arguments presented by Popper.

I think that Popper's most important contribution to the philosophy of history is to be found in his covering law model of explanation whereby an event is to be explained when it is subsumed under a covering or general law. The history of the covering law model remains unwritten, but while it is present in Hume and J. S. Mill and even, as I have argued elsewhere, in a passage in Aristotle's *Posterior Analytics,* its importance to contemporary philosophy of history derives from the treatment and refinement it has received first from Popper in *The Logic of Scientific Discovery* and later from Hempel in several articles. To judge from his recent intellectual autobiography, Popper regards his situational logic as being an even more important philosophical discovery than the covering law model of explanation, but this seems to me a case where a scholar has misjudged the comparative importance of his contributions. Even so, Popper's situational logic represents an ambitious attempt to preserve Collingwood's theory of sympathetic understanding while avoiding his subjectivism, and I believe that, should the current controversy concerning the covering law model ever subside, Popper's situational logic may well become the next most discussed topic in the philosophy of history. Even if this expectation is proven wrong, Popper's impact upon the philosophy of history will remain considerable. His attacks upon historicism, for example, clearly anticipate the arguments against historical determinism and its alleged connections with political totalitarianism which we find in Isaiah Berlin's famous and influential *Historical Inevitability,* and, while the question of influence is a subtle one, readers of this book will see that W. H. Walsh, John Passmore, Alan Donagan, and others have assimilated much of Popper into their own philosophies of history. Popper believes that, whatever the virtues of specialization may be elsewhere, specialization is the bane of philosophy, and I think his most enduring contribution to the philosophy of history may be that he has reminded us of its essential connections with the "larger issues" of freedom and determinism, the role of institutions in scientific and political development, and the moral meaning or significance of the historical process.

In this book I take exception to many of the things Popper has to say about the nature of historical investigation and hypotheses, and I disagree strongly with his claim that a theoretical science of society and history is impossible, but these differences must be seen against a background of shared assumptions: that there is a unity of method in the natural and social sciences, that scientific and empirical statements are falsifiable, and that there is a dualism between facts and moral standards.

CHAPTER ONE

The Question 'Has History Any Meaning?'

In the concluding chapter of *The Open Society and Its Enemies* Popper considers the question 'Is there a meaning in history?'. He begins with a disclaimer intended, I think, to distinguish his approach to this and other philosophical problems from that of analytic or ordinary language philosophers: "I do not wish to enter here into the problem of the meaning of 'meaning'; I take it for granted that most people know with sufficient clarity what they mean when they speak of 'the meaning of history' or of 'the meaning or purpose of life'."[1] I shall not deal directly with the problem of philosophical method in this book, but it should be noted that one could talk about meaning without talking about purpose, and the question of the meaning of history and the question of the meaning of life are not necessarily co-extensive. Popper might not deny either of these things, but since 'meaning' is not univocal it may be desirable, regardless of one's conception of the task of philosophy, to distinguish several different senses of

1. *The Open Society and Its Enemies* (London, 1966; Princeton, 1971), II, 269. This book was first published in London in 1945 and subsequently was revised, mainly with an Addenda written in 1961.

'meaning' before launching into a topic so broad as the meaning of history.

In this connection W. H. Walsh's paper, " 'Meaning' in History," is useful. Walsh argues that it is the historian's business to provide not just a plain narrative (or chronicle) but a significant narrative of historical events. He believes that the attempt to answer causal questions is what makes a narrative significant, but he notes that Aristotle correctly saw that the question of causation is complex. Accordingly, Walsh gives examples of explanations which historians provide and which, he believes, illustrate what Aristotle calls efficient, formal, and final causation, and in doing so he makes this point about explanation: "To explain is to render intelligible; it is to find meaning and point in material initially not seen to have meaning and point."[2] It is the causal explanation (in one or more of Aristotle's senses of 'cause') of events that informs us as to the meaning or point of the events in question.

Walsh then proceeds to distinguish between 'meaning in history' and 'meaning of history.' 'Meaning in history' is, he optimistically maintains, essentially nonproblematic. A historian who asks about meaning *in* history is asking for an explanation of some historical event. "That history is meaningful, i.e. intelligible in principle in the light of such explanatory procedures as we can bring to bear on it, is so far from being a matter of dispute that every historian assumes it. But of course those who claim that history has *a* meaning must do much more than repeat this comparatively uninteresting proposition."[3] Here Walsh tacitly but correctly assumes

2. " 'Meaning' in History," in *Theories of History,* ed. Patrick Gardiner (New York, 1959), 299.
3. Ibid.

that, while it is natural to search for a plurality of meanings *in* history, talk about the meaning *of* history usually involves the search for a single, unitary meaning of history. He observes that to search for a meaning or the meaning of history is to ask a question of no special concern to the historian: "Just as the fact that a scientist succeeds in understanding a set of previously puzzling phenomena is without relevance to the thesis that we can make sense of nature as a whole, so is the historian's activity of establishing order in his material irrelevant to the question of whether a pattern can be discerned in history."[4]

Where the meaning *of* history is concerned, Walsh believes that two distinct inquiries can be made. The first and more modest is the search for regular laws or patterns in history which govern all historical change. The second inquiry searches for what he calls "a single plot or pattern in the whole course of historical development. . . . history makes sense only if the goal in question is something of which we can morally approve."[5] Walsh also notes, "The moral overtones which are so characteristic of speculative philosophy of history in its classical form need not be present in an enquiry into the laws governing historical change, which could be conducted in a strictly scientific spirit."[6] There are then on Walsh's view one resemblance and two differences between these inquiries into the meaning of history. Both inquiries are concerned with finding the laws of history, but the second inquiry attempts to show both that "history is going somewhere" and that the goal in question is something of which we morally approve.

4. Ibid.
5. Ibid., 303.
6. Ibid., 304.

Surely Walsh is right in supposing that the first sort of inquiry into the meaning of history could, if successful, find laws of history without also telling us either where history is going or whether it is morally desirable that it is going where it is. All a law tells us is that under certain conditions certain events will—or will not—occur, and the question whether these conditions obtain is a separate matter. The prediction that certain events will occur (in this case that history is going in some specific direction) requires, according to classic covering law doctrine, the deduction of a statement that such events will occur from premises containing both a law or laws and a statement specifying that the initial conditions mentioned in the law do in fact obtain. As we shall see, there are problems concerning historical patterns or trends—do they exist and, if so, are they subsumable under laws just as other events are?—and in talking about where "history taken as a whole" is going—is there actually a whole of history and, if so, is it an object of empirical investigation, or is it problematic in the way that Walsh suggests "nature as a whole" is? For now, however, let us assume that whoever undertakes Walsh's first sort of inquiry into the meaning of history (presumably, if Walsh is correct, he will be a nonhistorian) could also use the laws of history he has discovered to tell us where history or the historical process is going, by joining to these laws statements that the conditions mentioned in the laws have in fact been satisfied. Also we can assume that whoever does Walsh's second kind of inquiry into the meaning of history (he, too, will be a nonhistorian) could inform us, legitimately rather than oracularly or prophetically, where history is going only by using the laws discovered by the first sort of inquirer. I believe, therefore, that the only significant difference between the two sorts of inquiry into the meaning of history is the moral difference Walsh has noted, and even here I doubt that moral *approval* of where history is going is necessary for the second sort of inquiry. Suppose, for example, that someone doing the second sort of inquiry is persuaded that history is moving away from individual liberty and toward a state of affairs in which privacy is as little allowed for as it is in Plato's *Republic,* and suppose further that he absolutely abhors all of this. Nevertheless, I don't think he thereby needs to find history devoid of moral meaning or significance. The meaning of history may be horrible or tragic, but horror and tragedy need not be meaningless from the moral point of view—and indeed tragedy insofar as we still distinguish it from horror or misfortune cannot be meaningless. In short, I want to suggest that it is the moral posture or the moral concern which marks the second sort of inquiry into the meaning of history. It is this moral concern which, I believe, guarantees that the philosophy of history is an ongoing, essentially open-ended affair that will not terminate if and when the problem of historical knowledge and the fate of the covering law model of explanation are resolved.

It might, of course, be objected that moral meaning is just one kind of meaning, that history has aesthetic or religious meaning as well. While history can be regarded in terms of its aesthetic or religious meaning, traditionally speculative philosophy of history has been mainly preoccupied with the question of the moral meaning of history. The reason for this seems to be that history is somehow a more appropriate object of moral concern than of aesthetic or religious interest. The quest for aesthetic meaning makes or expects too much of history: although history has its dramatic moments and its stories of adventure, the world of artifacts and the theater seems a more reliable source of aesthetic delight than the world of historical facts and documents could ever be. On the other hand, the quest for religious meaning tends to make too little of history by emphasizing the finitude, the frailty, and the disappointments of earthly existence: for Saint Augustine man's historical existence was justified as a source for the production of souls to enjoy an eternal (nonhistorical) existence. But if history lacks a sufficient number of heroes or saints to sustain an aesthetic or religious interest, no one could, I think, reasonably complain that it is lacking in moral problems of great urgency and universal concern.

Karl Popper raises the question, "*Is there a meaning in history?*" and answers it by saying that "*History has no meaning.*" He then qualifies this answer by claiming that, while history has no ends of its own, we impose our ends upon it: "*although history has no meaning, we can give it a meaning.*"[7] The significance of these remarks cannot be understood apart from Popper's anti-historicism, which will be one of the themes of this book; in this connection Popper, although he is a realist and not a Kantian in his theory of knowledge, takes what is essentially a Kantian position, and the Kantian aspects of his philosophy of history and of his ethics will be another theme in this work. Here it may be helpful to note briefly the resemblance between what Popper has said about the meaning of history and what Kant has said about the final end of history: Kant believed this idea or concept is not constitutive of the nature of historical reality but that it is nevertheless important as a regulative idea or concept which reflects our

7. *The Open Society and Its Enemies,* II, 269, 278.

moral concern with the course of historical development and which may also be of some heuristic value as an organizing principle in our inquiries concerning past events, and this is essentially the position Popper takes concerning the meaning of history. Also, as we shall see, Popper, like Kant, denies that history taken as a whole is knowable: Popper denies that history taken as a whole "exists," while in the Kantian terminology history in this sense is not an object of possible experience. Also, Popper, again like Kant, argues in favor of a fact-value dualism whereby moral decision-making, including our decisions to try and impose our ends upon history, is autonomous from any factual discoveries we may make in science, psychology, or history.[8] There is still debate over what Popper means by 'historicism' and the appropriateness of this terminology[9]; but it will, I think, prove helpful if we regard historicism as the denial, or the tendency to deny, the validity of the three basic positions that I have claimed Popper shares with Kant.

In *The Poverty of Historicism* Popper defined historicism as "an approach to the social sciences which assumes that *historical prediction* is their principal aim, and which assumes that this aim is attainable by discovering the 'rhythms' or the 'patterns', the 'laws' or the 'trends' that underlie the evolution of history."[10] In *The Open Society and Its Enemies,* in the

8. See my "Teleology in Kant's Philosophy of History," *History and Theory,* 5 (1966), 172–185.

9. For a useful clarification of Popper's anti-historicism and a defense of his choice of the word 'historicism' see Alan Donagan, "Popper's Examination of Historicism," *The Philosophy of Karl Popper,* ed. Paul Arthur Schlipp (La Salle, Ill., 1974), II, 905–924.

10. *The Poverty of Historicism* (London, 1961; New York, 1964), 2. This book was first published in London in 1957; it had appeared in article form in *Economica* in 1944 and 1945. *The Open Society and Its*

passage immediately preceding his discussion of whether history has any meaning, Popper noted, "Historicism is out to find The Path on which mankind is destined to walk; it is out to discover The Clue to History (or as J. Macmurray calls it), The Meaning of History."[11] In effect Popper is saying that historicism belongs to that second and more ambitious sort of inquiry into the meaning *of* history which Walsh (influenced in large part, I believe, by Popper) sought to clarify: historicism attempts to tell us where we are going and that where we are going is a morally desirable goal or end. In terms of the fact-value distinction, historicism goes one step further: it seeks not only to tell us where we are going and that where we are going is a morally desirable goal or end, but it also seeks to derive moral imperatives from the allegedly factual claim that history is going in a certain direction. In short, historicism tells us that the goal or end toward which history is moving is morally desirable *because* history is moving toward that goal or end.

I shall later discuss in some detail Popper's dissection of the alleged weaknesses of historicism, but here it may be useful to explore, in a brief, preliminary fashion, his position concerning the limits of historical knowledge. Historicism cannot tell us where we are going and cannot rightly claim to find the meaning of history because, according to Popper, historical inquiry is necessarily limited in certain respects. In *The*

Enemies was, according to Popper, an "unintended consequence" of *The Poverty of Historicism* which he began before *The Poverty of Historicism* was actually completed. For a discussion of the relation of the two works see Popper's "Autobiography," *The Philosophy of Karl Popper,* I, 90–91. This autobiography is reprinted in a slightly revised form as *Unended Quest: An Intellectual Autobiography* (La Salle, Ill., 1976).

11. *The Open Society and Its Enemies,* II, 269.

Poverty of Historicism Popper states three theses which are relevant to our present concern. (1) He defends the view that "history is characterized by its interest in actual, singular, or specific events rather than in laws or generalizations."[12] (2) He endorses the covering law model of historical explanation (though not by that name) and claims, rightly, to have expounded the covering law thesis before Hempel did. He emphasizes, however, that while historical explanation involves the use of "universal laws," these laws are "of little interest" and they "may be so trivial, so much part of our common knowledge, that we need not mention them and rarely notice them." When the historian uses theories, theories of the sociology of power, for example, he does so "as a rule, without being aware of them. He uses them in the main not as universal laws which help him to test his specific hypotheses, but as implicit in his terminology. In speaking of governments, nations, armies, he uses, usually unconsciously, the 'models' provided by scientific or pre-scientific sociological analysis."[13] (3) He argues that history, like the natural sciences, must be selective, "unless it is to be choked by a flood of poor and unrelated material." The way to avoid being choked by too much data, according to Popper, is to introduce a "preconceived selective point of view into one's history; that is, to write that history which interests us."[14] This is not, he insists, an invitation to twist facts until they fit into a framework of precon-

12. Ibid., 143.
13. Ibid., 145. For Carl G. Hempel's statement of the covering law thesis, see "The Function of General Laws in History," reprinted in *Aspects of Scientific Explanation* (New York, 1965), 231–243, and "Explanation in Science and History," in *Philosophical Analysis and History,* ed. William Dray (New York, 1966), 95–126.
14. Ibid., 150.

ceived ideas or to neglect facts that will not fit into such a framework; on the contrary, all available evidence that is relevant to our point of view should be considered carefully and objectively. Such selective approaches in history fulfill functions analogous to the functions of theories in science, and such approaches are sometimes taken for theories. Sometimes certain ideas inherent in these approaches can be formulated as testable hypotheses, whether singular or universal, but as a rule these approaches or points of view cannot be tested: "They cannot be refuted, and apparent confirmations are therefore of no value, even if they are as numerous as the stars in the sky. We shall call such a selective point of view or focus of historical interest, if it cannot be formulated as a testable hypothesis, a *historical interpretation.*"[15]

I shall have more to say later about selectivity and interpretation and the role of these concepts in *The Open Society and Its Enemies,* but here I wish to state briefly several general criticisms of the three theses that Popper advances in *The Poverty of Historicism.* Where the first thesis is concerned, it is undoubtedly true that historians are characteristically interested in actual, singular, or specific events, although actual events need not be singular or specific in quite the way that some philosophers of history, including Popper himself at times, seem to think. If Hegel did nothing else of permanent significance in the philosophy of history, he made, or should have made, us sensitive to the great variety of interests and points of view among historians. Hegel's treatment of "original

15. Ibid., 151. The reader may wish to compare Popper's "interpretations" with what Walsh speaks of as "metaphysics." See Walsh, 305. The difference between Popper and Walsh seems mainly terminological; and in any event neither author regards metaphysical statements as "meaningless," as the positivists did, but rather as irrefutable and hence unscientific.

history" and "reflective history" (with "reflective history" being subdivided into "universal history," "pragmatic history," "critical history," and "fragmentary history") is a useful reminder to beware of sweeping, simplistic characterizations of "what historians do."[16] For example, there are original histories concerned with particular events occurring more or less within the lifetime of the historian who writes about them, and there are universal histories that concern the "whole" of a nation's history or even of world history. In my judgment to characterize events so complex as either the Peloponnesian Wars or the development of Britain as being singular or specific would be informative only as a way of telling us that historians are not concerned with wars or nations in general but only with particular wars or nations. In other words, too much emphasis upon actual, singular, or specific events as the objects of historical inquiry may lead one to deny or downgrade the historian's interest in more general considerations, especially in the causal connections among the many events which usually make up the problem or the "whole" that the historian investigates.

While Popper does not deny the presence of general considerations in historical inquiry, his second thesis does, I believe, downgrade them unduly; he concedes that historians use universal or general laws, but he stresses the triviality and the uninteresting nature of these laws. He acknowledges that historians use theories, but what this amounts to is that historians, for the most part unconsciously, use a terminology with a theoretical dimension as, for example, when they use general concepts like 'governments,' 'nations,' and 'armies.'

16. See chap. 1 of my *Hegel's Philosophy of History* (Ithaca, N.Y., 1974).

Sometimes historians' points of view contain ideas that can be stated as testable hypotheses, but usually they are nontestable and are neither theories nor hypotheses but "interpretations." There is one basic difficulty in what Popper has said about the laws, concepts, and points of view of historians, namely, it is ambiguous. Is he simply describing the limitations of many histories, or is he saying that history as a kind of inquiry necessarily has these limitations? It could perhaps be argued that many laws used by historians are of no interest, that many of their concepts are theoretical but only unconsciously so, and that many of their points of view are only interpretations; however, Popper has not given us any reason to suppose that this is true of *all* the laws, concepts, and points of view historians use (this would surely be false, as he himself concedes in effect when he notes that some points of view contain ideas that can be stated as testable hypotheses). Still less has he given us any reason to suppose this is *necessarily* the case where most or all of the laws, concepts, or points of view used by historians are concerned. What keeps history from being sociology or some other social science is, as Popper emphasizes, the historian's concern (subject to the qualifications I have noted above) with "actual, singular, or specific events." Whether the laws, concepts, and points of views historians use in their explanations of these events are, respectively, trivial, only unconsciously theoretical, or nontestable cannot help us in deciding whether any given piece of work is to count as history, although of course such considerations may affect our judgment as to whether the work in question is a good or significant piece of historical writing. Even if most or all of the laws, concepts, and points of view used by historians to this date were limited in the ways Popper has indicated, some future historian (after reading Popper and Hempel or for some other reason) might decide to make use of more interesting or nontrivial laws, might become more conscious of the theoretical implications of the concepts he uses, and might take greater pains to formulate his hypotheses in a testable form; the results might count as *revisionary* history, but there is no good reason to suppose that they would thereby cease to be history.

Popper's third thesis in *The Poverty of Historicism,* that of the importance of what he calls "interpretation" in the writing of history, is developed more fully and with some disturbing implications in *The Open Society and Its Enemies,* so for now I wish simply to pose an initial question. Can Popper give us good reasons to believe that interpretation is more central or basic to historical inquiry than to scientific inquiry? If he cannot, this would indicate the presence of a paradox in his philosophy. Popper in his epistemology and his philosophy of science is a sworn enemy of relativism or *"The Myth of the Framework,"* which he regards as being "in our time, the central bulwark of irrationalism." He concedes that "at any moment we are prisoners caught in the framework of our theories; our expectations; our past experiences; our language. But we are prisoners in a Pickwickian sense: if we try, we can break out of our framework at any time. Admittedly, we shall find ourselves again in a framework, but it will be a better and roomier one; and we can at any moment break out of it again."[17] The possible paradox is this: is Popper an enemy of the Myth of the Framework in general only to

17. "Normal Science and Its Dangers," in *Criticism and the Growth of Knowledge,* ed. Imre Lakatos and Alan Musgrave (Cambridge, 1970), 56.

become in effect its champion where the writing of history is concerned? Interpretations are, after all, frameworks or the results of frameworks; and frameworks reflect the necessity of our being selective, a necessity common to all organized inquiry. History and science alike require interpretations or frameworks for the selection and explanation of data; and in his reflections on both historical and scientific inquiry there is evidence that Popper believes we are not necessarily imprisoned for life in any one framework. Although Popper's reflections on the limitations of historical knowledge are, as I shall try to show, extremely complicated, he does, however, seem to doubt whether historians can succeed, as scientists allegedly can, in determining whether a new framework will be "a better and roomier one." Indeed, what he says about historians' frameworks or points of view, and interpretations seen as emanating from these points of view, suggests that they are incommensurate with one another. If history is actually limited in this way, then the apparent paradox is quickly dissipated: one can without risk of inconsistency attach a greater importance to interpretation or framework in one kind of inquiry than in another if the distinguishing characteristics of the inquiries in question warrant this. If, however, Popper cannot show that interpretation or framework is more basic to history than to science and that historians are less able than scientists to determine the merits of alternative frameworks, what importance should we attach to his error? The relativist might argue that probably Popper is mistaken in believing that either in science or in history we can move "at any time" from one framework to another, and that certainly he is mistaken in his belief that in science we can know, or even reasonably conjecture, that one framework is better than another.

In other words, what Popper has acknowledged, in effect at least, to be the case in history also obtains in science; and thus his error really consists in not having gone far enough in recognizing the incommensurability of frameworks. However, I shall argue from an opposed point of view, and one closer in spirit, I think, to Popper's own, that Popper has erred not in giving too much to science but in giving too little to history, and that this error results in the paradox of Popper's subscribing in effect to the Myth of the Framework in historical inquiry while repudiating it elsewhere.

CHAPTER TWO

Historical Interpretations

In *The Open Society and Its Enemies* Popper argues that, while history, like the sciences, must be selective, the ways in which history is selective differ significantly from what we find in physics, for example: in physics the point of view from which the selection of data is made is "usually presented by a physical theory which can be tested by searching for new facts. In history, the matter is not quite so simple."[1] Popper then proceeds to reiterate his support for what most philosophers, following William Dray, have come to refer to as the covering law model of explanation, but Popper suggests a distinction between what he calls "the generalizing sciences" and "the historical sciences." In the case of the generalizing sciences we are mainly concerned with universal laws or hypotheses; but in applied sciences such as engineering we are mainly interested in the prognosis: whether, for example, a bridge of a certain kind will carry a certain load. In such cases universal laws are means to an end and are taken for granted. Sciences that have this interest in specific events and in their explanation may, according to Popper, be called "historical sciences." He

1. *The Open Society and Its Enemies,* II, 261.

then writes, "from our point of view, there can be no historical laws. Generalization belongs simply to a different line of interest, sharply to be distinguished from that interest in specific events and their causal explanation which is the business of history. Those who are interested in laws must turn to the generalizing sciences (for example, to sociology)."[2]

In the above passage Popper is saying at once more and less than one might initially suppose. First, there is a more extended use of the word 'historical' than ordinary language would countenance, for all the applied sciences are lumped together with history as constituting the historical sciences—the mark of these historical sciences being not a common concern with the past but rather an interest in specific events, including, of course, specific events that are also past. This, so far as I am concerned, is a harmless technical innovation on Popper's part. At least, it is harmless so long as we realize that his claim that "there can be no historical laws" now means less than it might otherwise be taken to mean. It means that there are no historical laws in the sense in which there are also no engineering laws or medical laws as such: there may be laws of sociology which historians may use, laws of physics which engineers may use, and laws of chemistry and biology which doctors may use. What Popper is saying is that it is not the business or "line of interest" of historians, engineers, and doctors to seek to discover laws; their business concerns specific events. In one respect, however, Popper's claim that there are no historical laws has rather more bite where traditional issues in the philosophy of history are concerned. Given his views on the logical symmetry of explanation and prediction, his commitment to the unity of scientific method, and his opposition to

2. Ibid., II, 264.

all forms of historicism,[3] Popper's claim that there can be no historical laws can be reasonably taken to imply that there can be no *distinctively* historical laws, that is, laws which apply only to past phenomena and which can be discovered or understood only by historians or others specially trained in the study of past human events. In this respect Popper's extended use of the word 'historical' to include all the sciences interested in specific events serves the positive function of underscoring his rejection of a conception of historical inquiry as being *sui generis* or possessed of a methodology all its own. One way of summing up Popper's position on the alleged uniqueness of historical inquiry would be this: history has no distinctive subject matter; and if it did, this by itself would not make history a distinctive discipline with its own special method;[4] what history does have is an interest in specific or singular

3. I have in mind in particular his opposition to what he calls anti-naturalistic historicism, which he believes to be unduly concerned with the division of history into periods and with the emergence of novelty. See *The Poverty of Historicism,* 10–11. Later, however, I shall point out some significant resemblances between Popper and the anti-naturalistic historicist which Popper overlooked.

4. Such a view reflects an essentialism Popper has always condemned. "The belief that there is such a thing as physics, or biology, or archaeology, and that these 'studies' or 'disciplines' are distinguishable by the subject matter which they investigate, appears to me to be a residue from the time when one believed that a theory had to proceed from a definition of its own subject matter. But subject matter, or kinds of things, do not, I hold, constitute a basis for distinguishing disciplines. . . . *We are not students of some subject matter but students of problems.* And problems may cut right across the borders of any subject matter or discipline." Disciplines, according to Popper, are distinguished partly for historical reasons, partly for administrative convenience, and partly because the theories we construct to solve our problems tend to grow into unified systems, but all such classifications and distinctions seem to him comparatively unimportant and superficial ("The Nature of Philosophical Problems and Their Roots in Science," *Conjectures and Refutations* [London, 1963], 66–67). But see my footnote 89 in Chapter 4.

events, but the applied sciences are also interested in specific or singular events; thus, the important distinction to be drawn is not between history and the sciences but between history and the applied sciences on the one hand and the generalizing sciences on the other.

Popper writes that in the generalizing sciences theories or universal laws introduce unity as well as a point of view: "they create, for every generalizing science, its problems, and its centres of interest as well as of research, of logical construction, and of presentation. But in history we have no such unifying theories; or rather, the host of trivial universal laws we use are taken for granted; they are practically without interest, and totally unable to bring order into the subject matter."[5] It would be interesting, though for present purposes it is unnecessary, to speculate as to the standing of applied sciences such as engineering and medicine where this alleged contrast between the generalizing sciences and history is concerned. Are they, like history, condemned to a lack of unity and point of view? This would seem doubtful, since, although their interest is historical in Popper's technical sense of being concerned with specific events, Popper would scarcely be inclined to characterize the laws used by engineers and doctors as being trivial. (To do so would, of course, be one way of guaranteeing, though at an exorbitant price, the unity of scientific method: all the laws of physics, chemistry, biology, sociology, and psychology would now be considered equally trivial!)

But is it true that the theories or laws used by historians are "trivial" and "practically without interest" and "totally unable to bring order into the subject matter"? I noted above in connection with *The Poverty of Historicism* certain diffi-

5. *The Open Society and Its Enemies,* II, 264.

culties concerning Popper's allegations of triviality, and in my judgment Popper fails in *The Open Society and Its Enemies* to resolve these difficulties. He does, however, provide us with two examples of historical explanation. His first example concerns the division of Poland in 1772. If we explain this division by saying that Poland could not possibly resist the combined power of Russia, Prussia, and Austria, then "we are tacitly using some trivial universal law such as: 'If of two armies which are about equally well armed and led, one has a tremendous superiority in men, then the other never wins.' . . . Such a law might be described as a law of the sociology of military power; but it is too trivial ever to raise a serious problem for the students of sociology, or to arouse their attention." In his second example Popper does not even bother to spell out the "law" in question: he simply notes that "if we explain Caesar's decision to cross the Rubicon by his ambition and energy, then we are using some very trivial psychological generalizations which hardly ever arouse the attention of a psychologist."[6]

These examples do not, I'm certain, reflect the complexity we find in many historical explanations; and it is small wonder that, as Popper himself acknowledges, the attention of sociologists and psychologists would fail to be aroused by the universal laws that are used, whether tacitly or not, by historians in Popper's two examples. The fact that their attention would not be aroused suggests that there is something suspect about Popper's examples. Popper, of course, does not state that the universal laws or explanatory principles used by historians can come only from the theoretical sciences; the point I wish to make is that in the two examples he has given they obviously

6. Ibid., II, 264, 265.

do come from elsewhere and thus do not illustrate his thesis concerning the theoretical sciences as being at least one important source of the universal laws or explanatory principles historians use. If Popper, or anyone, believes that the laws of the theoretical sciences which historians might use in their explanations are necessarily trivial, this could be refuted by a consideration of virtually any of the sociological, political, and economic laws that he gives (for other purposes) on page 62 of *The Poverty of Historicism,* for example, 'You cannot have full employment without inflation,' or 'You cannot introduce agricultural tariffs and at the same time reduce the cost of living.'

Nevertheless, the problem of the alleged triviality of the laws or explanatory principles historians use, or might use, has some deep ramifications. Two suggestions made by Alan Donagan should be noted: first, an explanation may be trivial in the sense of being obvious without also being trivial in the sense of being unimportant; and second, what Popper has taken to be trivial empirical generalizations are really analytic truths.[7] Donagan's first thesis commands ready assent, but the second thesis is more difficult to evaluate. If true, it would explain why Popper has insisted upon the triviality of the laws and explanatory principles used by historians, since nothing could be more trivial than an analytic truth; and yet it would also explain why Popper insisted upon the presence of an element of universality in the explanations used by historians, since nothing could be more universally true than an analytic truth. Donagan, in his overall position, seems willing to accept the covering law model as an account of explanation in the

7. "The Popper-Hempel Theory Reconsidered," in *Philosophical Analysis and History,* ed. William Dray (New York, 1966), 146–150.

natural sciences, but in the case of historical explanation he has kept only the deductive requirement of the covering law model while rejecting its nomological requirement. According to Donagan, nobody doubts that some sociologists have set forth hypotheses that purport to be universal laws: "What has been doubted is whether any of them are true. The existence of false sociological hypotheses cannot show that there are true historical explanations which rest on covering laws."[8] But why has Donagan retained the deductive aspect of the covering law model, and why does he believe that analytic truths play an essential role in historical explanations? Since his proposal is an original[9] and significant variant on the covering law model, it may be useful to quote in detail a passage in which he provides a clearly stated example of what might be called Donagan's deductive-analytic model of historical explanation:

It is not difficult to show that historical explanations satisfy the deductive thesis. Suppose an historian explains Brutus's decision to join Cassius's conspiracy by saying that Brutus has resolved to preserve the Republic at all costs, and judged that the logic of his situation was that only by his joining Cassius could the Republic be preserved. Those who object that this involves the law, *All men who resolve to achieve a certain end at all costs, and who judge that only by doing a certain act can it be achieved, will do that act,* forget that laws must be empirically falsifiable. What they allege to be a law is in fact an analytic truth; for if a man has refrained from a certain act which he

8. Ibid., 146.
9. It was first stated, I believe, by Donagan in his *The Later Philosophy of R. G. Collingwood* (Oxford, 1962), in a more modest form when he wrote that some of the "closed hypotheticals" used by historians are "analytic truths" (191).

judges to be necessary to a certain end, it immediately follows that, when he refrained, he was not resolved to achieve that end at all costs. He might once have been so resolved, and have lost his resolution; but that is something else. Hence the statement that Brutus was resolved at all costs to preserve the Republic immediately entails the singular hypothetical: *If Brutus judged that to preserve the Republic it was necessary to perform a certain act, he would perform that act.* From this hypothetical, together with the statement of initial conditions, *Brutus judged that to preserve the Republic it would be necessary to join Cassius's conspiracy,* you can deduce the *explanandum* that *Brutus joined Cassius's conspiracy.*[10]

This passage, while suggestive, poses numerous difficulties. No one could, I think, reasonably deny that analytic truths may be present in or presupposed by the explanations historians provide,[11] but after this the going becomes increasingly difficult. Donagan's point about analyticity seems ambiguous in much the same way that Popper's point about triviality seems ambiguous: is Donagan claiming that historians could never use valid, universal psychological or sociological laws in their explanations because no such valid laws could ever be found, or is he simply stating the more restricted and less interesting thesis that no such valid laws are presently available

10. "The Popper-Hempel Theory Reconsidered," 150.

11. The same is undoubtedly true of some of the explanations scientists offer, a fact which helps account for the view still prevalent in some quarters that the laws of nature are analytically true. In this connection see Ernest Nagel's discussion of the statement 'Copper is a good electrical conductor' in *The Structure of Science* (New York, 1961), 54–55, 66–67. Nagel makes the interesting point that this statement was once asserted on experimental grounds but now serves to convey a logically necessary truth: high conductivity is now taken as a "defining property" of copper. I do not mean to claim that Popper's "psychological generalizations" have been similarly transformed into Donagan's "analytic truths," but rather to suggest that such transformations are possible.

for historians to use? I think he is arguing the stronger thesis, but if so it seems counterintuitive to suggest that, since the general premise or premises upon which historians' explanations depend are analytic truths, the only way in which empirical error could be present in a historian's premises would be in his statement of initial conditions and that if these conditions are correctly stated (and assuming, of course, that a historian knows an analytic truth when he sees one), there can be no disputing a historian's explanation of an event. I should think historical explanation sufficiently complex that making a mistake in explaining historical events could be more interesting than Donagan's position would seem to allow.

Perhaps what is ultimately at issue in disputes of this kind is the viability of the distinction between analytic and synthetic statements. Some philosophers complain that the analytic-synthetic distinction is intolerably vague, but the same philosophers often remark that if statements such as that given in Donagan's '*All men who resolve . . .*' example are analytic truths, then they are analytic truths of a peculiar kind, since they suggest a necessary logical connection between thought and action. This criticism suggests that those who are bothered by the vagueness of the distinction know how to use it well enough to be troubled by analytic truths with empirical consequences. Let us consider in some detail Donagan's example of an analytic truth, '*All men who resolve to achieve a certain end at all costs, and who judge that only by doing a certain act can it be achieved, will do that act.*' A person who doubted this truth would, Donagan must believe, be ignorant of the meaning of the concept 'resolve,' or fail to understand what 'resolve to achieve a certain end at all costs' involves, namely, a commitment to action, or at least a commitment to action when one who is so resolved also entertains certain beliefs about the appropriateness of a certain act to the achievement of the desired end. But, of course, it is notorious that men do not always act to carry out their resolutions even when they believe that a given act will bring about whatever it is that they seek to realize. Donagan tries to show that any demur to the analytic truth in question which might be based upon such considerations would be irrelevant: "if a man has refrained from a certain act which he judges to be necessary to a certain end, it immediately follows that, when he refrained, he was not resolved to achieve that end at all costs. He might once have been so resolved, and have lost his resolution: but that is something else."[12] But is this so? Is a man afflicted with "weakness of will" a man who has lost his resolve, at least temporarily, or is he a man who is unable to act upon his resolve? Also, there are difficulties concerning exactly what it means to be resolved to achieve a certain end "at all costs": it must mean something different in the case of a struggling student who resolves to become a doctor at all costs and in the case of Brutus. Even in the case of Brutus, while there it clearly means that Brutus is willing to give up his life to save the Republic, is he willing to do this only if he is certain he can actually kill Caesar, or is he willing to if he believes he has a good chance of killing Caesar or that he has only a fair chance of killing Caesar? I am not questioning the obvious logical relation between 'resolve' and 'commitment to act,' but I am suggesting some ways in which people who are not ignorant of the meaning of 'resolve' can seriously go about doubting the "analytic truth" in question, which gives us reason to suppose that it is not analytic or not analytic "in

12. "The Popper-Hempel Theory Reconsidered," 150.

the usual sense." We might, of course, attempt to preserve the bridge between mental state and overt behavior in Donagan's example, by using qualifiers like 'normally' or 'other things being equal,' but such qualifiers are conspicuously absent in our traditional examples of analytic truths.

Various possibilities suggest themselves at this point. We might take the line that some analytic relation between thought and action is necessary but not sufficient to explain the action in question (actions are usually taken to be intentional, and intentions are always or usually intentions to do certain things, but intentions may "misfire" in a number of ways). Or we might say that Donagan's claim is at present hard to assess: until we have "analytic truths" such as Donagan's point about 'resolve' and its connection with action presented in a comprehensive theory about human behavior, it will not be clear exactly what part, if any, these seemingly special truths play in the explanation of human behavior. Donald Davidson makes the radical suggestion that it is mainly because "we cannot see how to complete the statement of the causal conditions of intentional action that we cannot tell whether, if we got them right, the result would be a piece of analysis or an empirical law for predicting behavior."[13] But Davidson's despair over spelling out the ways in which beliefs, desires, or attitudes must cause action is accompanied by the certainty that "empirical laws" for predicting behavior will not be exact or strictly lawlike if they seek to explain overt physical behavior in terms of the mental: "We know too much about thought and behavior to trust exact and universal statements

13. "Freedom to Act," in *Essays in the Freedom of Action,* ed. Ted Honderich (London, 1973), 154.

linking them."[14] Davidson's arguments for this claim, however, are holistic and a priori (I am using these terms here descriptively and nonpejoratively). His case for what he calls the "holism of the mental realm" rests upon the claim that beliefs and desires result in behavior only as they are "modified and mediated by further beliefs, attitudes, and attendings, without limit,"[15] but this can only mean (1) that no single belief or desire is sufficient to account for even relatively simple instances of human behavior; (2) that beliefs, attitudes, and attendings we do not now have may modify the beliefs and desires we do have and consequently our future conduct; and (3) that the possible modifications of belief and desire and thus of behavior are "limitless" or infinite.

One could accept all of this, I think, without despairing over the possibility of discovering exact and strictly lawlike explanations of human behavior in terms of the mental, and indeed it seems fairly obvious that the sorts of considerations which lead Davidson to postulate the holism of the mental could also be used to establish an analogous physical holism. No single physical factor, for example, is sufficient to explain even relatively simple physical events, such as combustion; any single factor such as the presence of oxygen which does contribute to the event in question may be affected by the introduction of other variables, including more oxygen, with attendant changes in the quality and duration of the event in question; and the possible modifications of the factors which account for such events, and thus the possible modifications

14. "Mental Events," in *Experience and Theory,* ed. Lawrence Foster and J. W. Swanson (Amherst, Mass., 1970), 91–92.
15. Ibid., 92.

of the events themselves, are "limitless" or infinite. Indeed, arguments like this are often used to show not the impossibility but the *incompleteness* of explanations in the physical sciences; and it may be argued that Davidson's point about the limitations of psychological laws should be extended to *all* scientific laws as follows: it is impossible, or virtually impossible, to give all the necessary and sufficient conditions for any behavior, human or physical, but this does not prevent our predicting such behavior on the basis of empirical laws. The relation between incompleteness and inexactness would need further exploration, but there is, I think, no conclusive a priori reason to expect more inexactness in the case of laws about human behavior than in the case of laws about purely physical events.

Davidson, of course, would disagree, and the a priori element in his argument is explicit in passages such as the following: "Nomological statements bring together predicates that we know a priori are made for each other—know, that is, independently of knowing whether the evidence supports a connection between them."[16] In view of all the difficulties that attend Davidson's desire (a) to accept some version of the Identity Thesis while rejecting the possibility of exact psychological laws and (b) to preserve the fact (the freedom and causal efficacy) of human agency by insisting on the "Anomalism of the Mental," it is perhaps anticlimactic to suggest that Davidson's claim concerning how much we already know about the mental and the physical is the most troublesome. To concede, as Davidson does, that we may have true general statements relating the mental and the physical and that these statements may have the logical form of a law while maintaining that such statements could never be strictly lawlike (there

16. Ibid., 93.

will always be a "nomological slack" between the mental and the physical and this slack is "essential so long as we conceive of man as a rational animal")[17] seems arbitrary; and we do not know whether to be more impressed by what Davidson has granted or by what he has denied. In any case it seems precarious for rationality and free agency to hinge upon some unspecified nomological slack in as yet undiscovered laws: even if Davidson is right and some slack will always necessarily obtain, the amout of slack and hence the room left for rationality and free agency seems uncomfortably contingent. I shall return to some of the problems concerning human agency, freedom, and determinism, as treated by Popper, in Chapter 4.

Thus far I have argued against both Popper's claim that the empirical generalizations used by historians are (necessarily?) trivial and Donagan's suggestion that the apparent triviality of the explanatory principles used by historians stems from the fact that such principles are actually analytic truths.[18] It is *not* my intention in this study to undertake a comprehensive defense of the covering law model of explanation, but it may be apropos at least to indicate briefly what some of the

17. Ibid., 98.

18. Popper's own position on the analytic-synthetic dichotomy is that it "applies in a precise sense only to a formalized language, and therefore is liable to break down for those languages in which we must speak prior to any formalization, i.e. in those languages in which all the traditional problems were conceived" (*Conjectures and Refutations,* 74). According to Popper, a theory such as Newton's may be *"interpreted"* either as factual or as consisting of implicit definitions; thus for Popper the important consideration lies not in what a physicist might say on this point but in the attitude he takes toward tests which go against his theory. I shall discuss Popper's anticonventionalism in the philosophy of science in the final chapter, but it is clear that Popper himself chooses to interpret Newton's theory as factual and hence falsifiable.

major criticisms of it are and how seriously I regard them. A criticism advanced by William Dray, Michael Scriven, and others maintains that the business of explanation is to make things clear and that what counts as making things clear is context-dependent[19]—the upshot of all this is that explanation does not depend upon subsuming events under laws. But this pragmatic dimension of explanation may be granted, while a complete contextual relativization of explanation may be rejected. Even if the sole business of explanation were to make things clear, we might, in the spirit of Aristotle, suggest a distinction between being clear in the order of nature, and being clear in the minds of certain addressees; 'being clear in the order of nature' would serve as a reminder that just any kind of clarity in explanation will not do and that ultimately clarity cannot, or should not, be divorced from considerations of correctness. While philosophers such as Dray and Scriven wish to argue that the covering law model lays down too stringent a set of requirements for explanation, it is sometimes suggested that the requirements of Dray's and Scriven's conception of explanation are in a sense too lax, that any explanation will be incomplete until we arrive at entities that by their very nature require no further explanation by reference to things outside themselves. I think Aristotle and Hegel believed this, and in any event it is a challenge to the adequacy of both the covering law model as laid down by Popper and Hempel and the pragmatic or contextual conception of explanation

19. See William Dray, *Laws and Explanation in History* (Oxford, 1957), and "The Historical Explanation of Actions Reconsidered," in *Philosophy and History*, ed. Sidney Hook (New York, 1963), 105–135; and Michael Scriven, "Truisms as the Grounds for Historical Explanations," in *Theories of History*, ed. Patrick Gardiner (New York, 1959), 443–475.

provided by Dray and Scriven. Historical agents imperfectly and the historical process perfectly exhibit this requirement of ontological completeness, Hegel believed, and one finds traces of this attitude in Michael Oakeshott and others when they affirm the principle of historical continuity and deny that the category of causality can be, strictly speaking, a historical category.[20]

I am of two minds about this ontological model of historical explanation: while it seems useful as a reminder of the importance of human agency and of the independence of the historical process from extra-historical forces, it seems doubtful in that it sets the requirements for completeness in explanation too high. Since historical agents are only imperfect instances of ontological self-sufficiency or of things that are causes of themselves, we are driven back to the historical process itself as the ultimate element in any proper historical explanans, and thus we cannot be said to have explained any historical phenomenon until we have given all its antecedent conditions. Oakeshott, at least, reasons in this way when he argues for the principle of continuity and rejects the principle of mechanism or causation as a historical category. The method of the historian, according to Oakeshott, is never to explain by means of generalization but "always by means of greater and more complete detail," and, while Oakeshott does speak of "societies" or "social wholes" as the subject matter of history, this seems to violate his own principle of historical continuity and to invoke the method of generalization, at least as a way of differentiating one society or social whole from another. On

20. See Oakeshott, "Historical Continuity and Causal Analysis," in *Philosophical Analysis and History,* 192–212 (reprinted from Oakeshott's *Experience and Its Modes* [Cambridge, 1933]).

the seamless web view of history, any selection of subject matter is bound to seem arbitrary, and any explanation of that subject matter must seem incomplete. Indeed, once causality is rejected as a nonhistorical category, it is difficult to see what would count as an explanation of historical phenomena other than the piling of detail upon detail, and it seems doubtful whether fuller and fuller descriptions of events can ever be substituted for an explanation of such events. R. G. Collingwood's famous claim that in history when we know (in great detail, I suppose) what has happened we already know why it happened is either false or it can be made trivially true by including in our description of an event the explanation of that event, either overtly as in 'The American Civil War, which was caused by differences between the North and South over the institution of slavery, began in 1861 . . .' or tacitly as in 'Brutus, fearful over the fate of the Roman Republic, proceeded to stab Caesar. . . .' When causality is rejected as a nonhistorical category and when even Hegel's distinction between the essential (necessary) and accidental properties of historical events is discarded,[21] it seems that the only, or principal, thing left for the historian is the *narration* in ever greater detail of historical events. And this seems an unduly restrictive conception of what the historian does.[22]

Where the autonomy of human agency is concerned, per-

21. Oakeshott seemingly rejects this distinction in denying that any historical events are accidental, but Collingwood can be read as retaining it in his argument that thought is the "inside" of a historical event and that we cannot be said to understand a historical event without understanding the thought "behind" it.

22. See W. B. Gallie, *Philosophy and the Historical Understanding* (London, 1964); Arthur Danto, *Analytical Philosophy of History* (Cambridge, 1965); and Maurice Mandelbaum, "A Note on History as Narrative," *History and Theory*, 6 (1967), 413-419.

haps the most modern and sophisticated defense of this position is to be found in the argument that the reasons for an agent's action cannot be correctly spoken of as the causes of that agent's actions and that, while reasons in some noncausal sense may be said to "explain" actions, reasons cannot figure among the antecedent causal conditions in general causal laws that purportedly explain human actions. However, the strict distinction required by this argument between actions and bodily movements (which *can* be caused) seems doubtful, and, as Donald Davidson points out, defenders of such a position seem to demand that human actions be removed altogether from the realm of causality. I share Davidson's fear that if human actions are literally uncaused then they must be unintelligible as well; and, until this objection is met, it seems reasonable to assume that reasons can be included among the causal conditions of human actions.[23]

Two other objections to the covering law model need noting: (1) that covering laws explain kinds of events, not particular events, and (2) that probability laws or hypotheses cannot explain particular events since such laws only make the occurrence of certain kinds of events seem likely or probable rather than necessary.[24] The first objection seems well taken if it is read as requiring that a particular event must be shown to be an instance of a certain kind of event before it can be said to be explained by laws covering that kind of event, and if it requires also that a causal analysis of a particular event, in

23. See R. G. Collingwood, *The Idea of History* (Oxford, 1946); A. I. Melden, *Free Action* (London, 1961); and Donald Davidson, "Actions, Reasons, and Causes," *Journal of Philosophy*, 60 (1963), 685–700.

24. See Maurice Mandelbaum, "Historical Explanation: the Problem of Covering Laws," *History and Theory*, 1 (1961), 229–242; and Scriven, "Truisms as the Grounds for Historical Explanations."

terms of necessary *and* sufficient conditions, be given insofar as this is possible. The second objection shows, to use Scriven's provocative description, that individual events simply "rattle around" inside probability laws or hypotheses: explanations using probability laws are incomplete in the obvious logical sense that statements affirming that certain events or certain kinds of events have occurred cannot be deduced from them. Popper's worries about probability laws or hypotheses are reflected in his judgment that, although by virtue of their logical form probability laws or hypotheses cannot be falsified, we can nevertheless adopt a convention or decide to treat them as falsifiable; and I believe that probability laws are best regarded as halfway houses on the road to strictly general or universal laws. Still, something is better than nothing: who, as Hempel suggests, would not hesitate to enter a sickroom when he believes it ninety percent probable that anyone who does so will contract a contagious disease?

Ultimately many objections to the covering law model of explanation seem rooted in the suspicion that the subsumption of human actions under covering laws poses a threat to human agency and what used to be called "freedom of the will." In this connection it is not, I think, merely *ad hominem* to note that the two foremost advocates of the covering law model, Hempel and Popper, deny being determinists: for Hempel this seems to involve chiefly his claiming that an agent's beliefs and desires may be numbered among the causes of his actions, but for Popper it involves a full blown defense of "indeterminism," a defense I shall consider in Chapter 4. One other point needs noting here: it is obvious that there are warring or conflicting intuitions about what an explanation, especially a complete explanation, consists in. My intuitions, as I have indicated, are that the pragmatic model of explanation sets the requirements for explanation too low (and seems content at times simply to describe the uses of the concept 'explain'), while the ontological model sets the requirements, at least for a "complete" explanation, much too high. I believe, however, that explanations can be complete in the *logical* sense specified by Popper and Hempel, that is, statements about the occurrence of particular events can be deduced from premises containing at least one general or universal law and the further statement that the initial conditions mentioned in the general law do in fact obtain; and while I remain troubled by the tensions between human agency and the prediction or explanation of human actions using general laws, I provisionally endorse the covering law model as the only model that satisfactorily accounts for both the generality[25] and the factually informative nature of many explanations in both the physical and the social sciences.

I have argued in favor of Popper's covering law model of

25. Donald Davidson's "implied law" thesis, as presented in "Actions, Reasons, and Causes" and elsewhere, is perhaps an alternative way of accounting for the element of generality in some explanations. Davidson begins by arguing that we are usually "far more certain" of a singular causal connection than of any covering law, and that the claim that singular causal statements entail laws is ambiguous. Such a claim may be read as entailing some particular law *involving the same predicates* used in the descriptions employed in a singular causal statement, or as entailing merely that there exists a causal law instantiated by *some true description* of the phenomena referred to in a singular causal statement. The second interpretation can be defended without defending any particular law; and moreover, while Davidson believes that reasons, for example, are causes of action, he does not believe that the laws explaining a class of events such as actions will necessarily describe their causes using the concept 'reasons'—in fact he doubts, as we have seen, that such laws will ever be possible. There are, however, at least two difficulties with Davidson's proposal. First, while we may be more "certain" of the truth of many singular causal connections than we are of any or most covering laws, "certainty" presumably refers to a psychological state, and in any case our certainty may be misplaced. Second,

explanation, and I shall argue against his theory of historical interpretation; but first I wish to discuss a relatively neglected but significant aspect of his philosophy of history, namely, his account of the role of "situational logic" in historical inquiry. In *The Poverty of Historicism* Popper noted briefly that "there is room for a more detailed analysis of the *logic of situations.* The best historians have often made use, more or less unconsciously, of this conception: Tolstoy, for example, when he describes how it was not decision but 'necessity' which made the Russian army yield Moscow without a fight and withdraw to places where it could find food."[26]

Popper has attempted a more detailed account of situational logic in *The Open Society and Its Enemies* and in *Objective Knowledge.* In *The Open Society,* immediately following his two examples of trivial general laws, he writes, "(As a matter of fact, most historical explanation makes tacit use, not so much of trivial sociological and psychological laws, but of what I have called, in chapter 14, the *logic of the situation;* that is to say, besides the initial conditions describing personal interests, aims, and other situational factors, such as the information available to the person concerned, it tacitly assumes

---

while singular causal statements may "explain" in some pragmatic sense even when no law has been produced, and while the "generality" of explanation may be partially satisfied by the claim that some causal law, though perhaps one using a different set of concepts, can be produced to support a singular causal statement, this must remain a promissory note until such a law is actually produced. Then and only then will we be in a position to decide whether such a law, if it uses concepts different from those found in the singular causal statement in question, actually does explain "the same phenomenon." As we move from what Davidson calls "primitive" to "elaborate" explanations (or from prescientific to scientific explanations), the demand that we actually produce a particular covering law in support of a singular causal statement becomes more urgent and, in my judgment, more reasonable.

26. *The Poverty of Historicism,* 149.

as a kind of first approximation, the trivial general law that sane persons as a rule act more or less rationally.)"[27] What Popper calls "the trivial general law that sane persons act more or less rationally" can hardly on Popper's own account be considered more interesting than any of the other trivial general laws that he believes historians use. Of course, we must remember that it is only "a kind of first approximation," but it is not entirely clear what it is Popper thinks the historian is trying to approximate. Is it, for example, a more precise law in which man's rationality is said to explain causally why he behaves in certain specific ways? Would more precise formulation or refinement allow us to retain the generality we expect to find in a scientific law, causal or otherwise, or would the greater precision be attained at the expense of generality and simply by our learning more about what a particular agent thought about a certain situation (in which case we run the risk of merely redescribing or reconstructing his situation as he saw it)?

Popper would deny that situational logic is interested either in "psychological assumptions" (or laws) about the rationality of human nature or in simply reconstructing or re-enacting an agent's reasoning about a particular situation.[28] What Popper has in mind when he speaks of situational logic is, I believe,

27. *The Open Society and Its Enemies,* II, 265.

28. Donagan writes, "I agree with Popper that, fundamentally, historical explanations are explanations by 'the logic of the situation,' " but Donagan objects that "what a man does depends on the situation as he thinks it to be, rather than the situation as it is" ("The Popper-Hempel Theory Reconsidered," 147). As we shall see, this involves such a drastic departure from what Popper is seeking to accomplish with his situational logic, especially when it is conjoined with Donagan's denial that Popper's trivial general laws are laws at all, that Donagan's "agreement" with Popper seems less important than his differences.

essentially this: we construct with reference to "the logic of the situation" models of rationality by means of which we seek to assess the appropriateness or rational adequacy of an agent's response to what is to him a problematic situation calling for some decision or action on his part. This interpretation is supported by an earlier passage in chapter 14 of *The Open Society and Its Enemies:* "The method of applying a situational logic to the social sciences is not based on any psychological assumptions concerning the rationality (or otherwise) of 'human nature'. On the contrary: when we speak of 'rational behaviour' or of 'irrational behaviour' then we mean behaviour which is, or which is not, in accordance with the logic of that situation. In fact, the psychological analysis of an action in terms of its (rational or irrational) motives presupposes—as has been pointed out by Max Weber—that we have previously developed some standard of what is to be considered as rational in the situation in question."[29]

Popper's indebtedness to Weber and his theory of ideal types is evident also in his discussion of R. G. Collingwood's theory of historical re-enactment. In his essay, "On the Theory of the Objective Mind" (1968), Popper writes:

You will see that Collingwood lays great stress upon the *situation* closely corresponding to what I call the *problem situation.* But there is a difference. Collingwood makes it clear that the essential thing in understanding history is not the analysis of the situation itself, but the historian's mental process of re-enactment, the sympathetic repetition of the original experience. For Collingwood, the analysis of the situation serves merely as a help—an indispensable help—for this re-enactment. My view is diametrically opposed. I regard the psychological process of re-enactment

29. II, 97.

as inessential, though I admit that it may sometimes serve as a help for the historian, a kind of intuitive check of the success of his situational analysis. *What I regard as essential is not the re-enactment but the situational analysis.* The historian's analysis of the situation is his historical conjecture which in this case is a metatheory about the emperor's reasoning. [Popper is considering Collingwood's example of the Theodosian Code.] Being on a level different from the emperor's reasoning, it does not re-enact it, but tries to produce an idealized and reasoned reconstruction of it, omitting inessential elements and perhaps augmenting it.[30]

Situational analysis takes place on a different "level" from that of the thought processes of its subject matter. In the above example, the historian, according to Popper, seeks to produce an "idealized and reasoned reconstruction" of the emperor's reasoning which does not purport to correspond in all respects to what the emperor was thinking: inessential elements may be omitted, and the Emperor's thought may be augmented in various ways. Perhaps there is no difficulty in justifying the omission of "inessential" elements: this may be simply an unpacking of what it means to say that historical inquiry is necessarily selective. But there is, I think, something disturbing about 'omitting' when it is used in conjunction with 'augmenting,' especially when Popper does not explain what he has in mind when he speaks of augmenting the emperor's reasoning. Does he believe that the historian in doing situational analysis supplies, or should supply, missing steps in the emperor's calculations—in the way in which some historians of philosophy supply "missing premises" in the reconstruction of some philosophers' arguments? This may be a risky undertaking

30. *Objective Knowledge: An Evolutionary Approach* (London, 1971), 188.

even in the history of philosophy, and it is notorious that emperors are usually not philosophers and may not have proceeded carefully, step by reasoned step, in arriving at their decisions. The perils are even more obvious if 'augmenting' is taken to include the correction of steps in the emperor's calculations which the historian believes were illogical or erroneous. More seriously, there is the problem of what is the point or purpose of this idealized reconstruction of an agent's reasoning: is it the (causal) explanation of an agent's behavior or the assessment of the rationality of the agent's response to a problem situation that interests us? I think it is more the latter: Popper writes, "The historian's task is, therefore, so to reconstruct the problem situation as it appeared to the agent, that the actions of the agent become *adequate* to the situation."[31] Popper claims that, while this is very similar to Collingwood's method, it is devoid of the subjectivism that plagues Collingwood's theory of historical understanding.

On Popper's account, situational analysis seems to involve three things: first, there is an assessment of a situation by means of which we develop certain standards as to what would count as rational behavior in the situation in question; second, we develop a metatheory or an idealized reconstruction of the reasoning of the agent who confronts this situation; and third, we seek to assess the rationality of the agent's response to the situation in terms of the standards we have developed as to what would count as rational behavior in that particular situation. As we shall see, Popper believes that what the historian knows about a historical situation often depends entirely upon what an agent has told us about the situation in

31. Ibid., 189.

question. If this is so, there is the problem of to what extent, if any, the historian can arrive at an independent assessment of "the logic of the situation." On Popper's own account, the chances of his being able to do this would often seem none too good, and thus the historian's "metatheory" or idealized reconstruction of the agent's reasoning would seem to be of utmost importance. Here I must confess that I fail to see how a "metatheory" about the emperor's reasoning is any better off than a plain empathetic theory about the emperor's thinking: subjectivism seems a clear and present danger whichever description of the historian's activity we may prefer. Nor would it be enough to stress the idealized aspect of the metatheory, the omitting and augmenting that goes on, for Collingwood at least emphasized that all rethinking is critical rethinking. Still there is a difference: for all his emphasis upon the critical aspect of rethinking or re-enactment, it was explanation rather than assessment or evaluation which most concerned Collingwood. With Popper's situational logic, what we have essentially is an appraisal of the rational adequacy of the emperor's behavior, given what we know about his situation and his beliefs about his situation.

Popper's situational logic may, I think, help to clarify an appraising or assessing aspect of the historian's activity which is sometimes dismissed too lightly as "Sunday morning quarterbacking." In studying the conduct of a historical figure, the historian frequently forms his own beliefs about the logic of a problem situation confronting that figure, and even if these beliefs are formed solely or in large part in the light of testimony or evidence left behind by the agent in question, they need not coincide with the beliefs the agent himself actually held. The appraising or assessing the historian undertakes may have two or more dimensions. The rational adequacy of an agent's beliefs and behavior may be assessed, in a sense externally, and in terms that are at least tacitly comparative: did the agent view the situation as the historian has come to see it, and did his actions satisfy the historian's standards or decisions concerning what would count as rational or appropriate behavior in that situation? A second dimension of the historian's assessment is of a more "internal" nature in that the historian will be concerned chiefly with the consistency of an agent's behavior with that agent's beliefs: given that he believed as he did, was his behavior consistent with these beliefs? Was his strategy or conduct appropriate to the situation *as he saw it?*

In a sense the metaphors of 'external' and 'internal' might, if pressed too far, prove troublesome since, if I am correct, all appraisals or assessments of the rationality of conduct must take some cognizance of the beliefs an agent had about his problem situation and what he wanted to achieve in that situation; in this respect all such appraisals or assessments may be said to be "internal." What I could not understand or rationally conceive of would be an assessment of the rationality of an agent's behavior in cases where one had absolutely no knowledge or beliefs about how the agent conceived of his own situation; and, since I can conceive of an *explanation* of an agent's behavior in at least some cases where one has no knowledge or beliefs about how the agent conceived of his situation, it seems to me that the assessment of rationality is logically tied to "knowledge of other minds," whether this is got by empathetic understanding or by more ordinary means, in a way in which the explanation of behavior need not be.

What has Popper achieved in his remarks about situational

analysis? His intention, I think, was to show that historians characteristically do one thing: they explain particular events in terms of the logic of the situation and by the use, tacit or otherwise, of trivial general laws. His accomplishment, however, has been to show that historians do two things: they explain particular historical happenings by the use of general laws which need not be trivial; and they assess or evaluate particular acts or decisions in terms of standards of rational adequacy or appropriateness, arrived at in their situational analysis. One can only speculate as to why Popper has failed to appreciate the differences between explanation using general laws and assessment or evaluation using situational analysis. Perhaps the key lies in his emphasis upon the triviality of the general laws historians use. 'Sane persons as a rule act more or less rationally' is not very informative, and while Popper says it is a kind of first approximation, he doesn't follow this up, doesn't consider, for example, that it may be a first approximation to something like 'In a situation of type *c*, a rational agent will do *x*,' which in my judgment is clearly predictive rather than evaluative.[32]

One thing I find implicit in Popper's situational logic is the possibility of a new approach to the question, Should the historian pass judgment on the beliefs and actions of historical figures? It has usually been assumed that this question is primarily or exclusively concerned with *moral* judgment or evaluation and that the problem is basically whether the making of such moral judgments is part of or inimical to the historian's task of providing a reconstruction of the thoughts

32. This issue was subsequently explored in the debate between Hempel and Dray over whether rational appraisals in terms of 'the thing to do' could have explanatory or predictive import. See Hempel, *Aspects of Scientific Explanation* (New York, 1965), 469–472.

and actions of men who often held moral standards and ideals different from those held by the historian.[33] Popper, I believe, contributes essentially two things to this discussion: he reminds us in effect that not all evaluation is moral evaluation and that the problem of evaluation or judgment in terms of "alien standards" is perhaps not so critical for evaluation in terms of situational logic as it is for moral evaluation. Insofar as evaluating, assessing, or judging in terms of situational logic makes essential reference to the beliefs, and standards, of historical agents, the problem of "alien standards" is avoided in one crucial respect. To be sure, the historian's assessment of the situation and his conclusion as to what would count as rational behavior in that situation may not coincide with that of the agent he is studying; but at least it will be the agent's situation, his beliefs about and responses to that situation, which will be of primary concern to the historian who does "situational logic." Also, even if one believed that all moral questions are questions concerning rationality and even if one further conceived of this rationality using the most naturalistic construals of 'appropriateness,' no one, I think, would want to say that all questions about the rationality of various pieces of conduct were in any direct sense moral questions; and at least in cases where they were not, situational appraisals of appropriateness could proceed independently of moral evaluation.

Such considerations do not, of course, guarantee the correctness of a historian's conclusion as to whether an agent's beliefs or actions were appropriate to a given situation or even whether the action was consistent with the agent's own beliefs;

33. For an eloquent argument that moral judgment is inescapably part of the historian's task, see Isaiah Berlin, *Historical Inevitability* (London, 1954).

nor can such considerations guarantee that a historian's conclusions will be unaffected by whatever general prejudices or beliefs he may have as to what is prudent or foolhardy. In this respect rational evaluation or assessment in terms of the logic of the situation is not free from the pitfalls that moral judgment may encounter. However, if there are no knockdown arguments showing how rational evaluation can avoid the vicissitudes of moral evaluation, there may still be some differences worth noting. First, a case can be made that standards concerning what is to count as prudent or foolhardy are less affected by "cultural relativity" than standards as to what is to count as morally good or morally bad. Politics and logistics, for example, are the art of the possible in a way in which, it is at least arguable, morality is not; also, criteria for success in politics and war seem more obvious, and more universally agreed upon, than criteria for moral excellence. Second, rational evaluation in terms of the logic of the situation can, and usually does, rest content with an assessment of the rational appropriateness of certain means or strategies for the attainment of certain ends, while moral evaluation is often, if not always, concerned both with an agent's choice of means and the question of the goodness of the ends he pursues. Third, historians have no special training or competence qua historians for moral judgment or evaluation, and the few historians who have made a point of passing such judgments—Lord Acton, for example—usually seem to have benefited from an unusual religious or moral background more than from anything they may have learned from their historical exercises. Historians do, however, have special training and presumably competence in unraveling the moves and countermoves in complex activities such as politics and diplomacy, in at least *following,* and explaining, various and conflicting analyses of the logic of many, often practical, situations as such analyses were put forth both by historical figures involved in these situations and by other professional historians. Special training, of course, guarantees nothing, but it is not, I think, entirely accidental that in many societies a historical education has been regarded as a desirable preparation for careers in politics and diplomacy, for the analysis, in other words, of the logic of practical situations that politicans and diplomats may be expected to encounter.[34]

Historians explain events, and they sometimes assess the rationality of the beliefs and actions of historical figures; they also, according to Popper, employ "interpretations." In *The Open Society and Its Enemies* Popper's remarks about general laws and the logic of the situation read almost like a parenthesis in a text where the emphasis falls upon interpretations as being characteristic of historical inquiry and significantly different from anything we find in the generalizing sciences. Immediately after his discussion of the "triviality" of the general laws used in historical explanation and one brief comment concerning the logic of the situation, Popper writes, "We see, therefore, that those universal laws which historical explanation uses provide no selective and unifying principle, no 'point of view' for history." He concedes that to some extent a point of view is provided "by confining history to a history of something," for example, to the history of power politics or the history of technology. But as a rule further selective principles are needed, and these are provided by what Popper

34. See F. J. Levy, *Tudor Historical Thought* (San Marino, Calif., 1967), which traces the emergence of the idea that the historian should teach practical statecraft.

calls "preconceived ideas which in some way resemble universal laws, such as the idea that what is important for history is the character of the 'Great Men', or the 'national character', or moral ideas, or economic conditions, etc."[35] Popper insists, however, that such ideas or theories are "vastly different" in character from scientific theories:

For in history (including the historical natural sciences such as historical geology) the facts at our disposal are often severely limited and cannot be repeated or implemented at our will. And they have been collected in accordance with a preconceived point of view; the so-called 'sources' of history record only such facts as appeared sufficiently interesting to record, so that the sources will often contain only such facts as fit in with preconceived theory. And if no further facts are available, it will often not be possible to test this theory or any subsequent theory. Such untestable historical theories can then rightly be charged with being circular in the sense in which this charge has been unjustly brought against scientific theories. I shall call such historical theories, in contradistinction to scientific theories, *'general interpretations'*.[36]

I find this introductory argument in which Popper characterizes many historical theories as *"general interpretations"* troublesome, in part because it begins with a false or at least dubious assumption: "We see, therefore, that those universal laws which historical explanation uses provide no selective and unifying principle, no 'point of view' for history." The 'therefore' in this sentence was justified, Popper apparently believed, because of the alleged triviality of the universal laws that historical explanation uses. If, however, as I have suggested, such

35. *The Open Society and Its Enemies,* II, 265.
36. Ibid., 265–266.

laws need not be trivial, then the universal laws historians use might after all provide a selective and unifying principle or point of view, and thus the problem Popper is considering would not exist. Popper himself acknowledges that the "preconceived ideas" that meet the historian's need for further selective principles do "in some way" resemble universal laws, and in giving examples of such "ideas" he may have unintentionally provided us with some examples of nontrivial universal laws that historians use. Yet Popper also says that such ideas or theories as are provided by these further selective principles are "vastly different" in character from scientific theories; and we must now attempt to determine whether the resemblance or difference is greater.

First, we must locate the resemblance that Popper mentions but does not identify. The resemblance he has in mind stems, I believe, from the fact that the historical theories he cites purport to provide us with causal explanations of historical phenomena;[37] but this should count, especially to someone of Popper's persuasion, as a significant resemblance between such historical theories and those we find in science. Thus the difference Popper has in mind must be momentous: it cannot be, for example, merely that historical theories are less precise or less successful than their scientific counterparts. Before considering this difference, however, let me remark that Popper has put his finger on one aspect of historical writing which in my judgment stubbornly resists assimilation to either a scientific, explanatory model or an aesthetic, nar-

37. This is obviously true, for example, of Marxist theories that stress the causal importance of economic conditions, and it also seems true of "Great Men" theories of history. See Sidney Hook, *The Hero in History* (New York, 1957), especially 229, where the hero is spoken of as "an event-making individual who redetermines the course of history."

rative model. Regardless of whether the universal laws historians use are trivial or significant, no one could, I think, reasonably maintain that they provide, in full at any rate, a "selective and unifying principle," and thus I can to a point sympathize with Popper's looking elsewhere for such a principle or principles. It may be, however, that in looking for a "selective and unifying principle" we are seeking something so vaguely defined that we do not know exactly what we are looking for and hence would not recognize it if we found it; or it may be that, owing to the pervasive model of what allegedly occurs in the sciences, we undertake the analysis of historical activity with an overintellectualized or simplistic set of expectations. Perhaps when these expectations are disappointed, we refuse to concede that our quest was ill conceived, and we are tempted to say instead that historians use "general interpretations" and set out to prove this by noting the importance a historian appears to attach to Great Men or to economic conditions.

What, according to Popper, is the difference between the historical theories he has cited and those of science? Perhaps one key to the difference he has in mind lies in his repeated use of the word 'preconceived' ("preconceived ideas," "preconceived point of view," "preconceived theory") in characterizing the selective principles historians use. Ordinarily 'preconceived' has a pejorative ring to it, and this seems to fit Popper's intention here, as he is trying to show that history is limited in ways in which science is not. Popper is an anti-inductivist, however, and has repeatedly asserted that scientific theories are logically and temporally prior to observation and experiment. Thus, at least in the context of a discussion of scientific method, to say that a theory is preconceived might turn out to be simply a description or even a compliment when coming from someone of Popper's persuasion; and it is difficult to see how what is a plus where the sciences are concerned could become a minus where history is concerned. (In *The Poverty of Historicism,* 150, Popper notes in discussing the problem of selectivity that "initial conditions are very complex, and most of them have little interest for us." He recommends that "the only way out of this difficulty" is "consciously to introduce *a preconceived selective point of view* into one's history; that is, to write that history which interests us." Thus, it may be that one difference Popper has in mind is between preconceived points of view or theories that are *consciously* recognized as such and those that are not, but in recommending that historians consciously adopt a preconceived point of view, Popper in effect recognizes that this difference can be overcome.)

Although Popper could not, strictly speaking, argue consistently that historical theories, or at least those theories he calls "historical interpretations," are preconceived while scientific theories are not, he does maintain that they are untestable and that this untestability accounts for their being "vastly different" in character from scientific theories. The principal reason Popper gives in support of this claim of untestability has to do with the nature of historical evidence. The facts at our disposal are, first, "severely limited and cannot be repeated or implemented at our will," and second, "they have been selected in accordance with a preconceived point of view; the so-called 'sources' of history record only such facts as appeared sufficiently interesting to record, so that the sources will often contain only such facts as fit in with preconceived theory." The second statement shows, I think, what Popper may have had in mind in his frequent use of the word 'preconceived': historical theories are 'preconceived' in a double sense in that both the theories and the "facts" the theories purport to explain are preconceived. Historical "facts" come to us already interpreted, and the "sources" are not sources in the sense of giving us facts about the past as it really happened but only in the sense of reporting what these sources found interesting to record. The sources often contain only those "facts" that fit in with some theory, and we cannot test these "facts" because the events they report cannot be repeated at our will. I shall have more to say about this alleged untestability, but here three points need making briefly. (1) This is a small matter, but I doubt whether decisions as to what is interesting or worth recording need always or even usually be made on the basis of whether such "facts" fit in with some theory we hold. (Popper explicitly claims only that the sources will *often* contain only such facts as fit in with preconceived theory.) To maintain that this is always or even usually the case would, I think, be plausible only if we were to trivialize the notion of theory unduly, perhaps by using 'theory' in such a broad way that it now connotes 'whatever interests us.' Of course, whatever interests us may reflect some theoretical commitment on our part, but the sorts of things that get preserved in the historical record are often less sophisticated than what gets reported in even the simplest scientific observations, for example, letters to family or friends written by soldiers with no particular axe to grind or theory to sell. (2) It is sometimes pointed out in discussions of the relation of observations to theories in science that even if observation statements are made in the light of some theory, it need not be the same theory that they are used to test, and this remark seems especially apropos here. Thus, in the case of letters that a soldier writes home, even if such letters had a theoretical commitment, they might nevertheless help provide an "independent test" for the validity either of general theories or of particular hypotheses other than those the soldier in question subscribed to. A letter written solely to support the claim that its author handled himself well his first time under fire might provide evidence for the testing of some general theory about factors affecting the morale of the common soldier or some particular hypothesis to the effect that a certain retreat was an orderly withdrawal and not a rout. (3) That historical facts, or more precisely the events that such facts report or are "about," cannot be repeated could not be used as an argument against the possibility of historical knowledge. The reason for this is that the statement 'Historical events cannot be repeated' is a variant on 'The past is past' which is, of course, an analytic truth, and neither statement implies that *because* historical events cannot be repeated or *because* the past is past it is unknowable. Moreover, it is arguable that no events can be repeated if we take the notion of 'the same event in all respects' seriously or literally enough.

Popper in his remarks about the limitations of the historical facts available to us twice uses the word 'often' rather than 'always' or 'necessarily.' This suggests, I think, not that he intends to embrace historical skepticism, but rather that he is simply skeptical where many but not all historical "facts" are concerned. (A historical skeptic such as Jack W. Meiland would deny the possibility of *any* historical knowledge or even that we can, strictly or justifiably speaking, say that some historical statements are probably more well founded than others.)[38] Popper also acknowledges that all historical inquiries, including those of the "historical natural sciences," suffer from the same limitations: their "facts" cannot be repeated, and they have been collected in accordance with a preconceived point of view. But this acknowledgment amounts to more, I think, than Popper allows for. First, the historical natural sciences are rather numerous, and in any case we no longer have a distinction between science and history but between science on the one hand and history plus the historical natural sciences on the other. Second, the question arises as to how sharp a distinction we have here, of whether there is a *vast* difference between the facts available to historians, in Popper's broad sense, and to scientists.

Popper's basic complaint is that the historical sources often contain only such facts as fit in with preconceived theory and that *if* no further facts are available it will "often not be possible to test this theory or any subsequent theory." In the next paragraph he spells out this complaint further by noting that in history "we can rarely obtain new data able to serve as do

38. See his *Scepticism and Historical Knowledge* (New York, 1965). Meiland uses the claim that historical events cannot be repeated as a reason for accepting historical skepticism, but he has more sophisticated arguments. He asserts, for example, that no memory claims can be justified without the use of memory, but that some memory claims can be proved incorrect without the use of memory. However, this argument does not establish the asymmetry Meiland seeks: it does not show that any particular memory claim can be disproved without the use of memory, only that in cases where there are inconsistent memory claims at least one of these must be incorrect; and in cases where we have memories that exhaust all the possibilities in a given situation (Smith remembers that Jones was in the room while Black remembers that he was not), we can also know that one of these memories must be correct, although we may be unable, without the use of other memories, to say which one it is.

crucial experiments in physics."[39] I have two principal reactions to this: first, I doubt whether any difference as iffy or contingent as the one Popper has noted between the facts available to historians and the data available to physicists could establish that historical and scientific *theories* are "vastly different" in character; and second, even if it were true that the facts available to historians often were collected in the light of some preconceived theory and that frequently no further facts are available, it would not follow that it will "often not be possible to test this theory *or any subsequent theory*" (my italics). The most that would follow would be that the theory which was used to collect these facts could not be tested, and even this is problematic. It may seem plausible to maintain, for example, that if all we know about the state of mind or the intentions of a general is what that general chose to tell us, then we cannot independently test any of the theories or hypotheses he sets forth; this may in some cases be true, but things are not always so simple. "Internal evidence" in the form of inconsistencies and strange reticences or gaps in the record may lead us to doubt the theories or hypotheses an author or witness sets forth. Imagine that a general informs us that a particular campaign was intended only to divert enemy troops from the defense of a strategic city, but we note from the figures he has preserved that he committed more troops to this diversion than he had ever committed to any previous diversionary campaign and that he had made but slight preparations to attack the city in question. Imagine further that he omits to give, as he usually does, casualty figures for this campaign and that for unexplained reasons he delays for over a year in attacking the strategic city he claims was

39. *The Open Society and Its Enemies,* II, 266.

his principal objective. From these and similar considerations we might conclude, solely on the basis of internal evidence, that the diversionary campaign hypothesis is probably false, that the general in question had undertaken a major campaign that was either lost or fought to a bloody draw, leaving his forces too depleted for further significant action that year. It does not seem to be the case that facts collected "in accordance with a preconceived point of view" or because they are believed to "fit in with preconceived theory" could not in a significant number of cases be used to test that same preconceived theory; and indeed human frailty (the fact that witnesses frequently reveal more than they intend to) and the critical resources of the historian (the fact that he uses, in Collingwood's terminology, a question and answer method as opposed to a scissors and paste approach) suggest a more optimistic conclusion than the one Popper has reached.

As for Popper's stronger claim that it may often not be possible to test any *subsequent* theory, this would seem to depend more upon what that subsequent theory is like, how high-powered or ingenious it may be, than upon the limitations of available historical facts. In this connection Popper, I believe, has neglected the twofold or dual nature of historical observation. The facts available to historians are often records of observations made, if Popper is correct, in the light of theories; but these records are then observed by historians, also presumably in the light of theories. This brief depiction of the twofold or dual nature of historical observation, while obviously compatible with (and influenced by) Popper's insistence that all observation is theory-laden, suggests two things not noticed by Popper. (1) In cases where the theories the historian brings to the historical record are not the same as the theories initially used in the collection of the facts found in the record, there seems to be not even a prima facie reason to suppose that the facts in the records could not serve as an independent test of such theories, at least as independent, say, as the data used in crucial experiments in physics. (2) Strictly speaking, what the historian observes are records or artifacts and not facts. The question, What are historical facts? is a recurring difficulty in the philosophy of history, in part, I believe, because the word 'fact' has several different meanings, and, as most dictionaries recognize, can be used to refer either to events or to statements about events. Popper himself has already used the word 'fact' to refer both to events and to statements about events: when he wrote that historical facts cannot be repeated, I at least understood him to mean that historical events cannot be repeated (the repetition of statements about events would presumably pose no difficulties); and when he wrote that historical facts are collected, I understood him to mean that statements about events are collected or preserved in the historical records ('the collection of events' has, I think, no literal sense, at least not in the way that 'the collection of stamps' or 'the collecting of interesting guests' has). And, of course, a fact in the second sense is not simply a statement but a true statement (it is analytic that if a statement is a fact then it must be true). While Popper has already used 'fact' to refer both to events and to statements about events, he seems to have been entirely unaware of any shift in application, which may help account for the, in my judgment, undue emphasis he has placed upon the limitations of historical facts and the way his argument turns upon the absence of "further facts." I think that Popper's regret over the unavailability of further facts can be shown to be misplaced: if we take a historical fact to be a true statement about past events, then it is obvious that (a) not all the statements about past events which get preserved in the historical record are historical facts and (b) the number of true statements we can make about past events need not, and almost certainly will not, correspond to the number of historical facts contained in the historical record. If this is so, then the impossibility of repeating, or freshly observing, historical events does not rule out the possibility of our making fresh factual discoveries on the basis of a critical scrutiny of historical records or documents. Indeed, even if the historical record remains constant in the sense that no new artifacts or documents become available, it seems reasonable to assume that, as our methods of investigation and our insights into human behavior become more sophisticated, new factual discoveries will actually occur and that these facts may be used in the testing of various historical theories.

Of course, it might still be doubted whether or how the historian could come by theories different from those used in the collection of the "facts" already in the historical record, but this is a naive objection for which we can find a ready answer in Popper: such theories could be got from sociology or psychology, for example, or from any discipline (including other areas of historical inquiry) where independent testing *is* possible. And *how* the historian gets his theory is in any case irrelevant, if we agree with Popper that induction cannot be a significant source of scientific theories. Of course, the ultimate objection might be raised that no independent testing of any theory is possible, whether it be in history or in physics, and for the very reason Popper has noted, namely, that "observation is always *observation in the light of theories*" and that observation statements and experimental results are equally "interpretations in the light of theories."[40] I shall discuss this problem in the final chapter, but it is obvious that Popper would find this reading of the results of his philosophical investigations unacceptable, else he could scarcely use untestability to mark the difference between scientific theories and many historical theories, or the difference between science and anything.

My disagreement with what Popper has said thus far is of a piece with my objection to his claim that the general laws historians use are trivial. It is not that he is in all cases wrong, but rather that he is mistaken in maintaining that untestability is typical or characteristic of historical theories. Of course, it must be remembered that Popper's intention in all this is not to discredit the historian but to cut the ground out from under the historicist. His basic strategy is to attempt to steer a delicate course between putting history on a par with science, which is the great dream of pro-naturalistic historicism, and putting history down too far, to a point where there is no good reason for preferring one historical theory, law, or explanation to any other. Thus, while he has claimed that historical theories are often untestable, he has not claimed that this is true of all historical theories; and, as we shall see, he also wants to deny that all untestable historical theories or general interpretations are equally acceptable, or equally unacceptable, because this would give, if not a victory, then at least a license of sorts to historicist interpretations as being no worse than any other general interpretations of history.

40. *The Logic of Scientific Discovery* (London and New York, 1959), 59, 107. This work was first published in Vienna in 1934 as *Logik der Forschung.*

In discussing the untestability of historical theories or general interpretations Popper cautions us that "we must not think that a general interpretation can be confirmed by its agreement with all our records," and he points out that "there will always be a number of other (and perhaps incompatible) interpretations that agree with the same records." We must, according to Popper, give up "the naive belief that any definite set of historical records can ever be interpreted in one way only"; but he adds that "this does not mean, of course, that all interpretations are of equal merit."[41] Saying that they are not, however, poses the problem of how, once we have given up the "naive belief" in question, we can decide or choose among a plurality of competing (and possibly incompatible) but untestable historical interpretations. In this respect what Popper says about the confirmation of historical interpretations may initially mislead a reader unfamiliar with his overall position on confirmation and falsification, much as his earlier use of the word 'preconceived' may have misled a reader unfamiliar with his views on theory formation. In saying that general historical interpretations cannot be confirmed by agreement with all our records, Popper might appear to be singling out some deficiency peculiar to historical interpretations, but this is not the case since, according to Popper, no theory, whether historical or scientific, can ever be confirmed by agreement with "all our records." No universal statement or theory can be confirmed, Popper believes, because the number of possibly confirming instances of a universal statement or theory is infinite and because positive instances of a universal statement or theory can be collected at will and hence are of no value. In science when we say that one theory is

41. *The Open Society and Its Enemies,* II, 266.

better than another, we do not mean that it has been better confirmed by supporting evidence but that it is better "corroborated," i.e., that it has withstood severe tests which the competing theory has failed to withstand. But we must consider what, if anything, would allow us to say of a historical theory that it is better than its competitors when severe testing aimed at the falsification of such theories is rarely possible. (In history "a theory which can be tested and which is therefore of scientific character can only rarely be obtained.")[42]

Here it should be noted that Popper's problem differs significantly from that of a philosopher who believes that universal statements or theories can be confirmed in the sense of being shown to be probably true in the light of supporting evidence. At least such a philosopher would not regard the agreement of a universal statement or theory with "all our records" as being inconclusive in the way that Popper does, nor would he have difficulty in explaining the existence of a "number of other (and perhaps incompatible) interpretations that agree with the same records." To the extent that two or more interpretations do agree with the same records they are equally confirmed in that one respect, and their *incompatibility* (as opposed to mere difference) will be located elsewhere; in other words, they could not say truly incompatible things about the same records and be *equally* in agreement with the same records. Of course, there is a problem concerning "records," which is, I think, reflected in Popper's (unconscious) distinction between "records" and "data" when he writes that there may be a plurality of interpretations that "agree with the same records, and that we can rarely obtain new data able to serve as do crucial experiments in physics."

42. Ibid.

Although the words 'records' and 'data' are in many cases used interchangeably, there is one important sense in which one might reasonably maintain that records are at best "raw data" and that, properly speaking, the word 'data' may, or should, be used only to refer to true statements about phenomena such as historical events or scientific experiments, or to statements believed by an investigator to be veridical descriptions of such phenomena. In historical inquiry these statements will presumably be based upon a scrutiny of "all our records"—this at least is the ideal—but they certainly will not (always or even usually) agree with all the statements to be found in the historical record. (Obviously, this could not be the case where statements in the historical record conflict with one another, and it need not be the case where the historian doubts, on whatever grounds, the reliability of a historical witness. The historian is, of course, not restricted to a commentary, critical or otherwise, on statements actually contained in the historical record; he may, for example, make inferences about an event which no witness of that event ever made or recorded.) Perhaps the distinction between records and data could be put more clearly in terms of a distinction between documents and evidence (evidence being always evidence for or against some theory or hypothesis), but some such distinction would, I think, help us to locate more accurately than Popper has done what it is that historical theories or general interpretations should agree with. Agreement with the records becomes unimportant or misleading, I believe, unless this is understood to be elliptical for agreement with true statements about historical events based on a critical scrutiny of historical documents and artifacts. On this view critical scrutiny of the records in historical inquiry becomes analogous to a crucial experiment in physics, at least to the extent of making us doubt whether historical and scientific theories really are vastly different in character. And while there is an obvious connection between "data" (in the sense of true statements about past events) and "records" (in the sense of historical documents or artifacts) in that the existence of records is a necessary condition for the historian's knowledge of past events, limitations in the number, variety, and sources of the documents and other artifacts available to the historian do not carry over directly into specific limitations on what he can learn from a critical scrutiny of these documents and artifacts.

It might perhaps be asked, why is Popper so concerned with problems related to what Walsh would call "meaning in history" when he should be addressing himself more directly to what Walsh calls "the meaning of history"? In other words why is he considering whether history is intelligible in terms of explanations using general laws and whether historical theories or general interpretations are testable when, in the present context, it is clearly the moral meaning or significance of history he is interested in? The answer turns, I think, upon our recalling that Walsh distinguished not only between inquiries into meaning in history and inquiries into the meaning of history, but also between two sorts of inquiry into the meaning of history, one seeking to know the laws or the patterns of the whole of the historical process and the other seeking to know all that plus the moral meaning of the whole of the historical process. I do not know if Popper would accept the following characterization of historicism, but I propose that historicism can be regarded as a three-stage affair in which the success of our explaining particular events by subsuming them under laws is taken to be a good or even conclusive reason for believing that the entire historical process can be explained by subsuming it under either these same laws or some other laws of greater generality, and this in turn is taken to be a good or even conclusive reason to believe that we can discover the moral meaning of history taken as a whole. Popper, of course, would reject the argument I have attributed to the historicist: while acknowledging that particular historical phenomena are rendered intelligible by subsuming them under general laws, Popper denies that it makes sense to speak of the whole of history in the way that historicists allegedly do, and he denies, at least in *The Poverty of Historicism,* that there can be laws for any unique process, whether it be social or biological;[43] also he denies that moral meaning can be read off or inferred from any facts, including historical facts. While moral meaning is on Popper's view something that we bring into history, Popper would, I think, want to claim that bringing moral meaning into history is a more rationally defensible and worthy undertaking than, say, bringing moral meaning into a game of chance; and certainly he would want to claim that there are *illegitimate* ways, of which historicism

43. This, as we shall see, led him to question the so-called law of evolution, and it helps account for his rejection of evolutionary philosophies; but in his later work, especially "Of Clouds and Clocks" (1965), while still criticizing Darwinism as "tautological" and "imperfect," Popper has propounded in a tentative and highly speculative way an evolutionary theory of organisms as "a growing hierarchical system of plastic controls" in which the emphasis falls upon "problem solving" and "error elimination." He is fully aware of this change of position (see *Objective Knowledge,* 241), but perhaps not so fully aware of its implications for his philosophy of history. At least he has not recanted his argument from the uniqueness of the historical process to the impossibility of subsuming that process under general laws, and so I shall treat that argument as it was given in *The Poverty of Historicism.*

is a conspicuous example, of bringing moral meaning into history. For Popper historicism represents, I believe, a distorted expression of our need to know how we have come to have the problems we do and by what means we could proceed to resolve these problems. The need to know where we have been and even what options are now available to us (a prospective application perhaps of Popper's logic of the situation) *can* be legitimately met, Popper believes; and some meaning *in* history (some degree of intelligibility in Walsh's sense) is, I think Popper would agree, a necessary but *not* a sufficient condition for our being able to talk responsibly about the moral meaning or significance of history.

To sum up, there can be no history of 'the past as it actually did happen'; there can only be historical interpretations, and none of them final; and every generation has a right to frame its own. But not only has it a right to frame its own interpretations, it also has a kind of obligation to do so; for there is indeed a pressing need to be answered. We want to know how our troubles are related to the past, and we want to see the line along which we may progress towards the solution of what we feel, and what we choose, to be our main tasks. It is this need which, if not answered by rational and fair means, produces historicist interpretations. Under its pressure the historicist substitutes for a rational question: 'What are we to choose as our most urgent problems, how did they arise, and along what roads may we proceed to solve them?' the irrational and apparently factual question: 'Which way are we going? What, in essence, is the part that history has destined us to play?'

But am I justified in refusing to the historicist the right to interpret history in his own way? Have I not just proclaimed that anybody has such a right? My answer to this question is that historicist interpretations are of a peculiar kind. Those interpretations which are needed, and justified, and one or other of which we are bound to adopt, can, I have said, be compared to a searchlight. We let it play upon our past, and we hope to illuminate the present by its reflection. As opposed to this, the historicist interpretation may be compared to a searchlight which we direct upon ourselves. It makes it difficult if not impossible to see anything of our surroundings, and it paralyses our actions. To translate this metaphor, the historicist does not recognize that it is we who select and order the facts of history, but he believes that 'history itself', or the 'history of mankind', determines, by its inherent laws, ourselves, our problems, our future, and even our point of view. Instead of recognizing that historical interpretation should answer a need arising out of the practical problems and decisions which face us, the historicist believes that in our desire for historical interpretation, there expresses itself the profound intuition that by contemplating history we may discover the secret, the essence of human destiny.[44]

In the above passage Popper insists eloquently upon the practical significance and origins of our quest for viable interpretations of history. I should be inclined, however, to distinguish the question 'Which way are we going?' from the question 'What, in essence, is the part that history has destined us to play?'; although the two questions may seem to Popper to be the same or nearly so, this need not be the case. The first question could, I believe, figure as part of a rational examination of current trends with an eye to the further question of which of these trends is most likely to persist, while the second question does seem irrational or highly metaphorical. Popper's views on historical trends will be examined in detail later, but while his objection to the belief in *absolute trends,*

44. *The Open Society and Its Enemies,* II, 268–269.

trends that are unconditional and irreversible, seems well taken, the question 'Which way are we going?' admits, I think, of answers in terms of relative (conditional and reversible) trends; the belief in the existence of such relative trends seems to me entirely consistent with a refusal to believe that history has destined or determined us to do *anything.*

Popper's claim in the above quotation that the historicist interpretation of history paralyzes action is a complex issue with psychological, historical, and logical dimensions, but I seriously doubt whether historicism taken as the belief that certain trends will persist absolutely does as a matter of psychological fact actually paralyze action. It might paralyze or inhibit somewhat the actions of people who are *entirely* persuaded that certain trends will persist regardless of what opposing steps they might consider taking, but historicism seems not to paralyze the actions of historicists who believe history is moving in the direction these historicists favor. Nor, I think, is there any conclusive reason to suppose that it should: the belief that the plums will eventually fall from the tree has seldom discouraged anyone who is hungry from shaking the tree, or attempting to climb it. Popper describes Marxist historicism as being "a peculiar variety of fatalism, a fatalism in regard to the trends of history, as it were,"[45] but while there is an element of truth in this, it does not show, as Popper seems to think, that historicism and activism are inconsistent with one another, or that historicism paralyzes action. If historicism is "a peculiar variety of fatalism," Popper has failed, I believe, to see just how peculiar it is when compared, for example, to religious fatalism. Religious fatalism does seem to follow from the doctrine of predestina-

45. *The Poverty of Historicism,* 51.

tion or the belief that the fate of each individual soul has already been determined and that there is nothing in the form of good works or anything else the individual can do to alter this; but what could historicist fatalism follow from? Even the most specific historicist prediction tells us nothing about the fate of particular individuals or the kind of society a given individual will live in. Accordingly, if a historicist claimed to know only what the general trends of history are and if the state of his "knowledge" (what he thinks he knows will happen) were the only relevant variable here, he could believe either that activism on his part might hasten the coming of socialism and thus increase the likelihood of his living in a socialist society *or* that activism on his part, while it will not hasten the arrival of socialism, is nevertheless necessary, given his historical situation, his temperament ("I have to do *something* even if it makes no difference, or even if the difference it does make is already predetermined"), and so on.

Of course, it may be pointed out that someone who believes in predestination doesn't know, or claim to know, the fate of his soul but this doesn't prevent his believing that God has already decided what it will be; by the same logic, the historicist might not know, or claim to know, whether he will someday live in a socialist society, but this needn't prevent his believing that the outcome has been or will be determined by "historical forces beyond his control." This may be correct, but presumably the ways of history are not as mysterious to the historicist as the ways of God are to the religious person, and the difference seems crucial. To use a distinction of Popper's, I should classify a person who accepts the religious doctrine of predestination as "a metaphysical determinist" (at least he believes that the fate of each individual soul is fully predetermined, even if he also believes in "freedom of the will" where human decisions and actions are concerned), but not as "a scientific determinist" (at least he makes no claim that *we* could in principle foretell the fate of any individual soul.)[46] Unfortunately, Popper does not explicitly relate his discussion of the two kinds of determinism to historicism, but I think he would be inclined to regard the historicist as both a metaphysical and a scientific determinist.

Although I have some doubts about such an interpretation or reading of historicism, I shall for the rest of this section argue that, even if it were correct, historicism is, or could be, consistent with activism. If a historicist did believe that in principle we could know the future, including his future, in its smallest detail, he must admit that in fact we do not have this kind of knowledge at present. Thus, while he may believe on what he regards as scientific grounds that socialism is inevitable, that the trend toward socialism is irreversible and even unconditional, and while he may be, as Popper suggests, a fatalist in this respect, this is no reason for him to be a fatalist in the sense of passively awaiting the victory of socialism. Given the present state of historicist theory and the data available to him, the historicist has no way of knowing whether he will eventually live in a socialist society, but also he has no way of knowing whether he will passively await the coming of socialism or work actively for it. Thus, while he may believe (a) that his decision in this matter is entirely predetermined, (b) that in principle at least it could be known in advance, and (c) that foreknowledge of what people will do even when it is self-referential is not problematic, this position

46. For Popper's distinction between metaphysical and scientific determinism, see his "Indeterminism in Quantum Physics and in Classical Physics," *British Journal for the Philosophy of Science,* 1 (1950), 117–133 and 173–195.

is equally compatible with either activism or passivity on his part. The only thing a historicist could not consistently believe, if he is also a metaphysical determinist, would be that activism on his part would in any literal sense *hasten* the coming of socialism or alter the (predetermined) time of its arrival. The realization that this belief could not be rationally entertained might dampen the enthusiasm of some historicists, but the historicist who remembers that he is also a metaphysical determinist will understand that this dampening of enthusiasm in some historicists is, like everything else, fully predetermined.

Another way of putting my point is this: scientific determinism is irrelevant in the case of a particular historicist seeking to decide whether or not to be an activist, since we, and the historicist in question, do not in fact know in advance how he will behave or what sort of society he will eventually live in; and metaphysical determinism, which simply maintains that everything is fully predetermined, has no practical consequences and accordingly is compatible with whatever an individual may decide to do. Therefore, while the individual historicist may be in a strong sense fatalistic where the trends of history are concerned—he thinks he knows both that they are predetermined and *what* they are—he cannot be equally fatalistic or fatalistic in the same sense where the details of history, including his own historical role, are concerned—he may believe that they, too, are fully predetermined but he doesn't know what *they* are. Not knowing in advance what his historical role will be, the historicist can without inconsistency embrace activism, without surrendering either his belief that this decision was predetermined or his belief that in principle this decision could have been foretold.

I shall have more to say about determinism later, and I shall defend a "soft" determinism as being necessary if we are to make sense even of Popper's own "three-worlds" doctrine; but for now I believe that I have shown how in terms of internal consistency an historicist could be a metaphysical determinist, a scientific determinist, and an activist, and that Popper is mistaken in affirming that historicist interpretations of history "paralyze" action.

Popper believes, despite what he has said about the circularity of historical interpretations, that some historical interpretations may be needed and even justifiable. In the long passage I quoted above from *The Open Society and Its Enemies* he spoke of "interpretations which are needed, and justified, and one or other of which we are bound to accept." In science we would, I believe, be disinclined to choose between theories which are for whatever reason untestable; and if, as Popper believes, we are "bound to accept" some historical interpretation or other, the necessity in question would presumably come from the direction of practice, perhaps from a genuine human need, rather than from the direction of theory or science. Popper at least reproaches the historicist for failing to realize that "historical interpretation should answer a need arising out of the practical problems and decisions which face us." However, if, as Popper believes, the choice among historical interpretations should be a rational and informed choice, then he must show that there is some rational ground or basis for preferring one historical interpretation to another. Since the alternative would seem to be an extreme voluntarism that would allow one to bring *any* meaning into history, including a meaning favored by the historicist, we must examine in some detail Popper's reasons for claiming that all interpretations are not of equal merit.

Popper writes, "First, there are always interpretations which are not really in keeping with the accepted records."[47] His initial effort to show an interpretation might prove to be unacceptable could be illustrated, somewhat drastically, by our trying to conceive of a *history,* or interpretation, of events which are not mentioned in any historical records and which have left behind no other evidence, in the form of artifacts or changes in the physical environment, that they ever occurred. However, in view of what Popper has said about how things *do* get included in the historical record, the fact that there are "accepted records" proves either too little or too much: it proves too little if it shows only that the records in question are judged to be authentic and not forgeries; and it proves, obviously, too much if it is used in support of any particular interpretation or interpretations. Given what Popper has said about the circularity of evidence and theory in historical interpretations, the fact that there are accepted records hardly provides a good reason for us to *reject* those interpretations which are "not really in keeping with" the accepted records. If anything, one might suppose that, on Popperian grounds, such theories or hypotheses are to be preferred over those which are in keeping, or agreement, with the accepted records. Theories or hypotheses not in keeping with accepted records can scarcely be said to be plagued by that circularity which is characteristic of historical interpretations in Popper's technical sense: some of them might even turn out to be falsifiable, which is Popper's great *desideratum.* And if by "not really in keeping with the accepted records," Popper means that

47. *The Open Society and Its Enemies,* II, 266.

such interpretations have in fact been falsified, then, strictly speaking, they are not interpretations in his special sense.

"Secondly," Popper writes, "there are some [interpretations] which need a number of more or less plausible auxiliary hypotheses if they are to escape falsification by the records; next there are some that are unable to connect a number of facts which another interpretation can connect, and in so far 'explain'. There may accordingly be a considerable amount of progress even within the field of historical interpretation."[48] This argument runs afoul of the same objections I raised in connection with Popper's first effort to provide us with reasons for preferring one historical interpretation to another; and it is in any case disconcerting to see the argument shift in the way that it does. His effort to show that not "all interpretations are of equal merit" occurs on the very page that began with his introduction of the term 'general interpretations' to refer to untestable historical theories, and where he argues, as we have seen, that confirmation by agreement even with all our records proves nothing, a claim that reflects both his skepticism about the worth of "confirming" any theory, be it scientific or historical, and his concern over the circularity of evidence and theory which plagues most historical theories. Now if a theory is to be testable, and if confirmation counts for nothing even in the case of theories that are testable, then testability must turn on falsifiability; but for Popper historical interpretations are untestable and hence unfalsifiable. Therefore, when he speaks of historical interpretations which "need a number of more or less plausible auxiliary hypotheses if they are to escape falsification by the records," he has either forgotten his own definition of a historical interpretation as

48. Ibid.

"untestable" or else he has used the word 'interpretation' in a different sense. In either case, what he has offered is not helpful in our effort to discriminate rationally between two or more untestable or unfalsifiable theories. In other words, historical interpretations in Popper's special sense are unfalsifiable, regardless of any help they may receive from "more or less plausible auxiliary hypotheses." In the final chapter I shall consider the role of auxiliary hypotheses in both the confirmation and the falsification of scientific theories, as well as Popper's criticism of the conventionalist strategy of trying to save a theory from falsification by the ad hoc introduction of more or less plausible auxiliary hypotheses. Popper's third point, that some interpretations cannot connect and explain a number of facts which another theory can connect and explain suggests that a more comprehensive interpretation is to be preferred over a less comprehensive one, and, other things being equal, this is surely true. But here the question must again arise as to how we can justifiably maintain that one interpretation can better connect and explain the facts if that interpretation is untestable, and Popper's use of quote marks around 'explain' indicates perhaps that he is aware of this or some related difficulty.

Popper's fourth suggestion is that "Furthermore, there may be all kinds of intermediate stages between more or less universal 'points of view' and those specific or singular historical hypotheses mentioned above, which in the explanation of historical events play the role of hypothetical initial conditions rather than of universal laws. Often enough these can be tested fairly well and are therefore comparable to scientific theories."[49] However, some of these

49. Ibid.

"specific hypotheses" closely resemble, according to Popper, those "universal quasi-theories" which he calls "interpretations," and these hypotheses are called by Popper "specific interpretations." Specific interpretations face the same problem of circularity confronting general interpretations: "For the evidence in favour of such a specific interpretation is often enough just as circular in character as the evidence in favour of some 'universal point of view'. For example, our only authority may give us just that information which fits with his own specific interpretation. Most specific interpretations of these facts we may attempt will then be circular in the sense that they must fit in with that interpretation which was used in the original selection of facts."[50] The distinction between specific or singular historical hypotheses and more universal points of view or general interpretations reflects Popper's initial claim that historians are more interested in particular events than in general theories. I agree with this and also with his claim that "often enough" specific historical hypotheses can be tested fairly well and therefore are "comparable to scientific theories."[51] Popper has failed, however, to give us *any* reason to be more optimistic where the testing of specific historical hypotheses is concerned than where the testing of general historical theories is concerned; and, since he notes that specific historical hypotheses, like general historical theories, may be affected by the problem of "circularity," optimism in the case of specific historical hypotheses would seem to be a kind of special pleading on Popper's part *unless* he can convince us that there is a more profound difference between general historical theories and specific historical

50. Ibid., 267.
51. Ibid., 266.

hypotheses than simply the difference between the general and the specific. He might, given his preoccupation with circularity, be tempted to try to make out some difference between the sorts of data available for the testing of general historical theories and specific historical hypotheses; but I am at a loss as to how such a difference could be established, since the same data may figure in the testing of both. Without some epistemic basis for a distinction between general theories and specific hypotheses we seem left chiefly with conflicting intuitions: Popper's intuition that general historical theories are rarely testable but that specific historical theories are testable "often enough" to resemble scientific theories; my intuition that general historical theories and specific historical hypotheses are equally testable and testable often enough to resemble scientific theories, at least to the extent of blocking Popper's claim that there is some great difference between science and history; and perhaps the skeptic's intuition, which is simply an extension of Popper's point about circularity to cover all historical theories and hypotheses. In any case, even if specific historical hypotheses are more often testable than general historical theories, Popper's concern should be restricted at this point to showing—since he believes that all historical interpretations are not of equal merit—how we can rationally decide if *any* untestable historical interpretation, be it general or specific, is preferable to any other.

Concerning the problem of circularity involving specific interpretations, Popper writes, "If, however, we can give to such material an interpretation which radically deviates from that adopted by our authority (and this is certainly so, for example, in our interpretation of Plato's work) then the character of our interpretation may perhaps take on some resemblance to that of a scientific hypothesis."[52] This suggestion seems at odds with Popper's very first proposal concerning how certain interpretations could be shown to be unacceptable: there are, he wrote, always interpretations which are "not really in keeping with the accepted records." While this proposal was made prior to Popper's discussion of specific hypotheses and interpretations, I fail to see how Popper could in the case of general interpretations recommend in effect that we discard an interpretation not in keeping with the accepted records while recommending in the case of specific interpretations that we take seriously an interpretation which deviates radically from the one adopted by our authority. I doubt that the distinction between general and specific amounts to much in the present connection, nor do I think it noteworthy that Popper in his first proposal spoke of interpretations which are not in keeping with "accepted records" and that he is now speaking of interpretations which clash with those accepted by some "authority." Presumably by "authority" he means some previous commentator(s), for example on Plato, but given his views on circularity I doubt whether Popper could, or would wish to, argue for an epistemologically or methodologically significant distinction between records (or texts) and authorities (or commentators). Earlier in connection with his remark that there are some interpretations not in keeping with the accepted records, I suggested that on strictly Popperian grounds this should be considered a plus for such interpretations rather than a minus, and now, with his own interpretation of Plato in mind, Popper seems in effect to be arguing in a similar manner. In any event, this entire business of whether an interpretation that "radically deviates" from

52. Ibid., 267.

accepted interpretations is for that reason closer to being, or being like, a scientific hypothesis is troublesome. Of course, the short answer is that to the extent a historical interpretation does actually resemble a scientific hypothesis then to that extent it must be considered testable; and if it is testable, then it can no longer be considered an interpretation in Popper's technical sense. But Popper's announced preference for historical interpretations which deviate radically from accepted interpretations and which must in this respect be considered improbable must be regarded as an instance, however imperfect, of his explicitly stated, general preference for improbable theories and hypotheses. Popper writes, "My theory of preference has nothing to do with a preference for the 'more probable' hypothesis. On the contrary, I have shown that the testability of a theory increases and decreases with its *informative content* and therefore with its *improbability* (in the sense of the calculus of probability). Thus the 'better' or more 'preferable' hypothesis will, more often than not, be the more improbable one." He then proceeds to deny that he has ever offered an improbability criterion for the choice of scientific hypotheses: "not only do I have no general 'criterion', but it happens quite often that I cannot prefer the logically 'better' and more improbable hypothesis, since someone has succeeded in refuting it experimentally."[53] I shall discuss Popper's rejection of all so-called "criterion philosophies" in the final chapter, but here it seems fairly obvious that his claim that it often happens that he cannot prefer the more improbable hypothesis since it may have already been refuted is something of a non sequitur, since his preference for the more improbable hypo-

53. "Conjectural Knowledge: My Solution of the Problem of Induction," *Objective Knowledge*, 17.

thesis concerns, or should concern, chiefly the selection of hypotheses deemed worthy of severe testing. Read in this way Popper's preference for improbable hypotheses or theories is open to the following objection raised by J. Bronowski: I am, he complained, a little out of patience with the exchange of gestures between Popper and those who think we can calculate the probability of a theory's being true, "but that may be because I am plagued more than Popper by people who send me improbable and silly theories."[54]

Popper's vulnerability to the sort of objection Bronowski raised is, I believe, a direct consequence of Popper's refusal to believe that a theory is confirmed, or probably true, when it explains all we know. Popper's final remark, in the paragraph in which he has attempted to provide, if not criteria, then good reasons why one historical interpretation may be preferred over some other, is that "it is a very dubious argument in favour of a certain interpretation that it can be easily applied, and that it explains all we know." This, he cautions, is often overlooked by "admirers of the various 'unveiling philosophies', especially by the psycho-, socio-, and historio- analysts."[55] He might have added: and by the advocates of induction and confirmation theory. I shall have some things to say in the final chapter about the alleged asymmetry between confirmation and falsification, but I shall not in this study undertake a detailed examination of Popper's essentially Humian denial that induction is rationally defensible; it should, however, be noted that one can be (as I am) an anti-inductivist where the formation or origin of theories is concerned without being

54. "Humanism and the Growth of Knowledge," *The Philosophy of Karl Popper,* ed. Paul Arthur Schlipp (La Salle, Ill., 1974), I, 620–621.
55. *The Open Society and Its Enemies,* II, 267.

committed to anti-inductivism where the testing of a theory or interpretation is concerned. In the present context, since Popper's desire to show that all historical interpretations need not be considered equally meritorious (or equally suspect) arises from his conviction that he has shown that historical theories are as a rule vastly different in character from scientific theories, it is important to note that he concludes by putting his finger on a problem which, if he is correct, affects both scientific and historical theories, namely, that it is the easiest thing in the world to apply such theories, that is, to find confirming instances of them.

One might wonder about some tension or possible inconsistency between this point and Popper's previous complaint about how severely limited the "facts" available to historians often are, but I shall assume that this is not a serious problem. I do, however, believe that Popper's basic position yields a result which, where the philosophy of history is concerned, is paradoxical or strongly counterintuitive. Popper can be read as saying in effect that in history we often have little or no evidence which can be said to support directly a particular theory or interpretation, and the evidence we do have is often circular with the theory or interpretation it allegedly supports, but that this is all right because in history as in science it really does not matter how much evidence we have in favor of a theory or interpretation; and the more outré the theory or interpretation, the more it departs from accepted accounts or the judgment of "authorities" the better, because it *risks* more. But while he seems to believe that any or virtually any historical theory or interpretation could conceivably be falsified by the discovery of new data, a person putting forth an especially farfetched theory or interpretation might believe that the chances of our discovering such new data are rare, at least according to Popper, and that his chances of being detected are therefore slight. Moreover, such a person could, in the event that new data do emerge, insist that such data only appear to support a previously accepted theory or interpretation, that all data are data or evidence only in the light of some theory or interpretation, and so on. This, I believe, calls attention to a basic difficulty in Popper's philosophy of history: how can we distinguish the heroic investigator who risks much from the charlatan who claims much, believing that the risk of his being found out is quite small? In science Popper's preference for improbable theories could be justified along these lines: we know exactly what a scientific theory risks, namely, falsification, and the more improbable the theory the greater the number of its potential falsifiers. But the greater the number of its potential falsifiers the more a scientific theory can be said to explain, at least until such time as it is in fact falsified. In science I think it not unreasonable to *recommend,* as Popper does, what might be described as a maximum risk/maximum gain strategy, although such a strategy seems to depart markedly from what actually occurs in what Thomas Kuhn speaks of in *The Structure of Scientific Revolutions* as "normal science"; however, this rather strenuous recommendation or prescription seems defensible in large part because Popper ties improbability so closely to testability and hence falsifiability. But surely there are special problems in the case of historical interpretations, which Popper characterizes as untestable and hence unfalsifiable; here the preferences for any such untestable theory or hypothesis on the basis of its improbability, where improbability is conceived of in terms of deviation from what is accepted by "our authority," would seem unwise. It would, for example, seem to provide some justification for any historicist interpretation that happens to deviate from what is accepted by "our authority," and this would surely be for Popper an unacceptable consequence of his preference for the improbable.

Immediately prior to the long passage quoted above in which he speaks of the "right" of each generation to frame its own interpretations of the past and in which he nevertheless denies the legitimacy of historicist interpretations, Popper advances the claim that while interpretations of the past may be incompatible with one another this is not necessarily the case. Whether it is the case seems, in Popper's judgment, to depend ultimately upon whether we can regard such interpretations as "crystallizations of points of view":

I said before that interpretations may be incompatible: but as long as we consider them merely as crystallizations of points of view, then they are not. For example, the interpretation that man steadily progresses (towards the open society or some other aim) is incompatible with the interpretation that he steadily slips back, or retrogresses. But the 'point of view' of one who looks on human history as a history of progress is not necessarily incompatible with that of one who looks on it as a history of retrogression; that is to say, we could write a history of human progress towards freedom (containing for example, the story of the fight against slavery) and another history of human retrogression and oppression (containing perhaps such things as the impact of the white race upon the coloured races); and these two histories need not be in conflict; rather they may be complementary to each other, as would two views of the same landscape seen from two different points.[56]

56. Ibid. Earlier in *The Poverty of Historicism,* 150–151, Popper had spoken of historical interpretations as being points of view rather than as crystallizations or expressions of points of view.

While the distinction between "interpretation" and "point of view" may not be altogether clear, it is, I think, fairly easy to see what Popper is driving at and even to agree with him that many interpretations, including some which appear to be at odds with one another, are not necessarily incompatible when seen as crystallizations or expressions of points of view. What this passage does, however, is to shift our interest from the question of what to do when two interpretations *are* incompatible with one another to the more serene prospect of a plurality, if not of compatible interpretations, then of compatible "points of view." Such points of view may be valuable aids in the production of histories that, while emphasizing different aspects of man's condition in the past, may nevertheless be "complementary to each other." Here we have an emphasis upon what Kant called the regulative use of such points of view or perspectives and their heuristic role in the writing of histories concerning topics of moral or practical interest to man in his present condition, for example, histories of freedom and of oppression. But to speak as Popper does here and later of what is in effect merely the regulative use of such points of view is, again in effect, to admit that in Kantian terminology such points of view are not constitutive of—not discoveries about—the nature of historical reality, or that if they are constitutive of the nature of historical reality, we have no way of knowing that this is so. (Here we can recall how seldom, according to Popper, we find the equivalent of a crucial experiment in historical inquiry.) At least this is my reading of what Popper has to say about incompatible interpretations and compatible points of view; ultimately the only way I can make sense of what Popper has claimed is to think of points of view as being somehow on a different "level" from interpretations. If, on the level of interpretations, I say that man is steadily progressing toward the open society and you deny this, then we are setting forth incompatible interpretations; but if, on the level of points of view, we say the very same things, then what we are saying is not necessarily incompatible. According to Popper, historical interpretations at least purport to be discoveries about the world, but points of view are rather ways of looking at the world. Since Popper has claimed that both general and specific historical interpretations are untestable, what he is offering us here is a way of living with this state of affairs and getting on with the business of writing history. The recommendation is that we see seemingly incompatible interpretations as crystallizations of points of view which need not be incompatible and that, given our point of view, we proceed to write the history that interests us. A history of man's progress toward freedom and a history of human retrogression and oppression "need not be in conflict; rather they may be complementary to each other, as would be two views of the same landscape seen from two different points."

As I noted above, Popper's strategem here simply shifts our attention from cases of incompatible interpretations and histories to cases of compatible ones, for surely he is not proposing that *all* interpretations and histories could be regarded as compatible once they are seen as emanating from various "points of view." In the case of histories of freedom and of oppression, for example, such histories could, as Popper maintains, be complementary, but whether in fact they are depends, of course, upon the claims they make. If one history maintains that the past or some portion of it is essentially a story of freedom and another argues that this is not so, it is hard to see how an appeal to differences in points of view could make these positions any less opposed. Popper might object to the "essentialism" which is presupposed by the claim that the past or any portion of it is essentially one thing and not another; but the question can be put more neutrally in terms of whether freedom or oppression predominates in the past or some portion thereof, and this seems a legitimate question which in some cases admits of genuine disagreement and, perhaps, resolution as well.

What is most disturbing about Popper's emphasis upon untestable interpretations and general points of view is that the possibility of our knowing the past seems in danger of slipping away. In the light of what Popper has said about the circularity of historical theories, historical data or facts may be regarded as a function of historical interpretations, and these in turn appear to be a function of points of view. Where points of view are concerned perhaps the ultimate problem they pose is whether and in what sense they may be said to be views of the same thing. Is the world of the man who sees history as the story of freedom and that of the man who sees history as the story of oppression the same world, and are histories written from these two perspectives really two views of the *same* landscape, as Popper would have us believe? Of course, 'landscape' serves here only as a visual metaphor: we literally see a landscape and can view it from various physical positions, but we cannot "see" or "view" (directly observe) the past in this manner. There remains the comforting belief or prejudice of common sense, which Popper and I share, that the world of the man who sees history as the story of freedom and the world of the man who sees it as the story of oppression must after all be the same world, but Popper's account of the circularity of many historical theories and his emphasis upon points of view suggests to one reader at least that perhaps a literal application could be given here to Wittgenstein's remark in the *Tractatus* that "the world of the happy man is a different one from that of the unhappy man."[57]

Despite Popper's deep-seated aversion to both the *Tractatus* and the *Philosophical Investigations,* his "points of view" seem to resemble in some respects Wittgenstein's "forms of life": both are general and yet basic or fundamental, and, as with "forms of life," one of the most important relations that points of view have with one another seems to be incommensurability, rather than incompatibility. Be that as it may, Popper advises us to write those histories that interest us—we inevitably do this, if Popper is correct, so the only question must be whether we do it knowingly or naively—and what interests us is a function of our point of view. Popper recommends that we freely acknowledge the importance of interpretation and point of view and that we abandon "an inapplicable idea of objectivity," namely, that we can "present 'the events of the past as they actually did happen'."[58] This emphasis upon writing about what we find interesting from our point of view is, as Popper acknowledges in a footnote reference to Max Weber, another way of recognizing the role of values in our selection of historical problems.[59] Of course, in urging us to give up an "inapplicable idea of objectivity" Popper is not recommending that we give up the quest for objectivity, although I believe, *contra* Popper, that historical objectivity does depend upon our being able to present the events of the past as they

193489

57. *Tractatus Logico-Philosophicus,* 6.43.
58. *The Open Society and Its Enemies,* II, 268.
59. Ibid., 364.

actually did happen; also, Popper's insistence upon the role of values in the selection of historical problems is logically compatible with the claim advanced by Ernest Nagel and others that, while our values may determine our selection of the problems we consider worthy of investigation, they need not determine the content of our attempts to resolve these problems. Even so it is difficult to see how Popper could justify denying to the historicist, and especially to any generation that happens to be historicist in its general outlook, the right to write the history which interests them and which reflects their present moral or practical concerns. ("Each generation has a right to look upon and re-interpret history in its own way, which is complementary to that of previous generations."[60] But *is* it complementary when a new generation consciously seeks to become radically discontinuous with previous generations?) There may well be a "need" for histories or interpretations written with various moral or practical concerns in mind; but, since Popper takes a dim view of "psychologism" or any psychological assumptions about "human nature,"[61] the important thing about such a "need" must be for Popper its social or cultural significance. In other words, in a situation (such as ours) in which cultural pluralism prevails, the "need" in question will express itself as a manifold of quite different needs. Historicists may simply turn out to be people with needs that are different from ours or Popper's: people who need to feel in tune with the times, people who are fearful of the future and afraid to venture out of doors without first ascertaining which way the winds of change are blowing, and so on.

60. Ibid., 267.
61. Ibid., 96–99; *The Poverty of Historicism,* 152–159.

While Popper might readily agree that historicists have needs different from ours, he would, I'm sure, refuse to let the matter rest there: historicists have beliefs about the past and expectations concerning the future which in Popper's judgment are not rationally justifiable. Still one might be somewhat surprised at the vehemence with which Popper attacks historicist interpretations of history, since he believes that (a) historical interpretations are untestable, (b) such interpretations may be complementary when seen as crystallizations of points of view, (c) we write those histories which interest us and what interests us depends upon our values, and (d) values belong to the domain of convention rather than to the domain of nature. (As we shall see, Popper employs the distinction between "nature" and "convention" in expounding his thesis that we bring meaning, a convention, *into* history rather than discovering it there, as we would in the case of facts about nature.)[62] Popper would, of course, regard as unwarranted any expression of surprise or imputation of inconsistency concerning his attacks upon historicist interpretations of history; and he would, I believe, seek to trace the difficulty to a misreading of (d) above. Conventionalism where values are concerned does not on Popper's view imply arbitrariness as is commonly believed: "Nearly all misunderstandings [of the claim that norms are man-made] can be traced back to one fundamental misapprehension, namely to the belief that 'convention' implies 'arbitrariness'; that if we are free to choose any system of norms we like, then one system is just as good as any other."[63] In Chapter 4 I shall discuss Popper's insistence upon the dualism between nature and

62. *The Open Society and Its Enemies,* II, 278.
63. Ibid., I, 64–65.

convention, or as he variously expresses it, the dualism between "facts and standards," "facts and decisions," "facts and policies," and "propositions and proposals." For now, however, I want to emphasize that what I have just quoted Popper as saying about norms is what he has also said about historical interpretations: that just because we are free to choose among them, it does not follow that any choice we might make is as good as any other. What Popper has done is to deny that the appeal to facts (whether they be facts about the past, facts about human or social needs, or facts about human norms or values) can decide our choice among historical interpretations. This is significant because he is here in effect rejecting the following argument, which one can imagine some ethical naturalist might set forth if he were asked what to do about "untestable historical interpretations": if, as Popper alleges, we cannot choose among historical interpretations on the basis of facts about the past, we can nevertheless avoid arbitrariness or skepticism concerning such interpretations by the appeal to facts of a different sort, either to facts about human or social needs or to facts about what human values prevail at a given time in some particular society; such an appeal would answer the question of which historical interpretation is better on the ground that one interpretation is needed more or that it is more consistent with certain prevalent values. Popper does not think that such an argument could succeed, and so he must find other reasons for rejecting historicism as a way of interpreting the past.

Popper maintains, as we have seen, that all historical inquiry and interpretation is necessarily selective; and his argument against the legitimacy of historicist interpretations of the past depends ultimately, I believe, upon his claim that historicists do not comprehend that historical interpretation is selective or at least fail to grasp the significance of this: "there can be no history of 'the past as it actually did happen'; there can *only* be historical interpretations, and none of them final; and every generation has a right to frame its own";[64] and again, "the historicist does not recognize that it is we who select and order the facts of history, but he believes that 'history itself', or the 'history of mankind', determines, by its inherent laws, ourselves, our problems, and even our point of view."[65] Popper here is advancing (at least) four distinct claims: (1) there can be no history of the past as it actually did happen but only historical interpretations of the past; (2) all historical interpretations are selective; (3) no historical interpretations are final; (4) because of (1), (2), and (3) the historicist's claim that he has discovered the inherent laws of history is mistaken. I wish to comment briefly on these claims now, reserving a fuller discussion of (3) and (4) for the next chapter.

First, Popper has not in my judgment even begun to demonstrate the impossibility of our writing a history of the past as it actually did happen. What he has said about the selectivity of historical inquiry cannot show this, as selectivity and objectivity need be in no way mutually exclusive. (The relationship between selectivity and definitiveness is another topic, which I shall discuss in the next chapter.) In any case, Popper's claim that "there can be no history of 'the past as it actually did happen'; there can *only* be historical interpretations" appears overstated even in terms of his own system if we recall that Popper initially was careful to acknowledge

64. Ibid., II, 268.
65. Ibid., 269.

that not all historical theories or hypotheses were "interpretations" in his technical sense. Second, since all inquiry is selective, it is not informative and may actually be misleading to claim in the present context that all historical interpretations are selective, even if it were true that there can only be historical interpretations as opposed to histories of what actually did happen. Third, the claim that historical interpretations are not "final" is unclear: it may mean either that no historical interpretations are absolutely or finally true or that none can be proved true. I shall have more to say later about Popper's doctrine of verisimilitude in which he speaks of "higher or lower degrees" of verisimilitude or approximation to the truth; but since he explicitly states that the degree of verisimilitude of a theory or statement exists independently of the truth-value of that theory or statement and, therefore, does not require a multivalued logic (a logical system with more than two truth-values, true and false),[66] I do not believe that he means to say of a historical interpretation that if it is true it may nevertheless not be absolutely or finally true. Accordingly, I shall assume that he means to assert that no historical interpretation can be proved true; and this, of course, would follow from what he has said about the circularity of evidence and theory or hypothesis which is the defining characteristic of historical interpretations in Popper's technical sense. However, Popper also believes, on different grounds, that no scientific or historical theory or hypothesis can be *proved* to be true:

In science there is no *'knowledge'*, in the sense in which Plato and Aristotle understood the word, in the sense which implies finality; in science we never have sufficient reason for the belief

66. *Conjectures and Refutations,* 233.

that we have attained the truth. What we usually call 'scientific knowledge' is, as a rule, not knowledge in this sense, but rather information regarding the various competing hypotheses and the way in which they have stood up to various tests; it is, using the language of Plato and Aristotle, information concerning the latest, and the best tested, scientific *'opinion'*. This view means, furthermore, that we have no proofs in science (excepting, of course, pure mathematics and logic).[67]

While there may be special reasons why historical interpretations cannot in Popper's judgment be "final," finality, according to Popper, is impossible where any scientific or historical theory or hypothesis is concerned. Thus, again, it is not informative, at least not especially so, for him to say of any historical theories or hypotheses that they cannot be proved true. An even more general way of putting this point is to note that Popper is a "fallibilist" in his theory of knowledge, and his fallibilism must apply to all knowledge claims regardless of the subject matter or discipline they pertain to (ultimately, I think, even the "proofs" of mathematics and logic could not, on this view, be said to be final, at least not in the sense of being immune to further criticism).

Finally, I wish to comment, briefly for now, on Popper's fourth claim, that the historicist has failed to discover the inherent laws of history. I happen to think that this claim is probably true, but I fail to see how it could be true on the basis of Popper's claims (1), (2), and (3). The selective and fallible nature of scientific inquiry does not render false the scientist's claim to have discovered the laws of nature, and I fail to see how the selective and fallible nature of historical inquiry constitutes a refutation of the historicist's claim to

67. *The Open Society and Its Enemies,* II, 12–13.

have discovered the inherent laws of history. Let us assume that the laws of history will be causal laws: since the attainment of objectivity in the sense of what happened in the past may reasonably be considered a necessary condition for our discovering why it happened, Popper's first claim, that there can be no history of the past as it actually did happen but only historical interpretations of the past, would, if correct, be sufficient to show that the historicist's claim to have discovered the (causal) laws of history is mistaken, but I have argued that Popper has failed to establish (1). Of course, even if we could know the past as it actually happened and even if the historicist's claim to have discovered the laws of history were correct, it would not follow that *everything* the historicist might claim to know about how history determines "ourselves, our problems, our future, and even our present point of view" would be correct. The historicist, like many investigators before him, might claim more than the specific content of his discoveries would actually justify or support. Where the historicist and his alleged discoveries are concerned, we should be especially alert as to whether various predictions do actually follow from the laws in question; we should carefully consider whether predictions telling us that under certain conditions certain phenomena will (or will not) occur, have been transformed by the historicist, either from confusion or by design on his part, into dogmatic, unscientific utterances about "absolute trends"; and we should be concerned if he offers statements about trends, whether absolute or otherwise, as a sufficient justification for various moral imperatives about how we should adjust to historical change. I shall have more to say later about these problems, but for now I wish to note simply that it would not follow from the fact that the historicist has claimed too much for the discoveries that he has made, or could make, that there can be no discoveries at all where the laws of history are concerned.

It would, I think, be useful to consider the following exercise or examination question: suppose Popper had to choose between anti-naturalistic historicism and pro-naturalistic historicism, which would he choose? or if such a choice is inconceivable, which of these two varieties of historicism would he regard as being less in error? Initially, it might seem that Popper would prefer pro-naturalistic historicism. While conceding that there are some differences between the "methods of the theoretical sciences of nature and society," he writes, "But I agree with Comte and Mill—and with many others, such as C. Menger—that the methods in the two fields are fundamentally the same (though the methods I have in mind may differ from those they had in mind). The methods always consist of offering deductive causal explanations, and in testing them (by way of predictions). This has sometimes been called the hypothetical-deductive method."[68] Given the significance Popper attaches to the unity of method, this fundamental agreement between him and the pro-naturalistic historicist might seem to relegate the differences between them to the status of a family quarrel or at least to make it clear that Popper would prefer pro-naturalistic historicism over anti-naturalistic historicism. There are, however, complicating factors, some of which become evident in the progression in *The Poverty of Historicism* from the section entitled "The Unity of Method," to "Theoretical and Historical Sciences," to "Situational Logic: Historical Interpretation," and finally to "The Institutional Theory of Progress."

68. *The Poverty of Historicism*, 130–131.

The line of argument that concerns me here can be outlined as follows. Popper fully endorses the unity of methods of the *theoretical* sciences of nature and society, but then he denies that history is a theoretical science (the historian is interested in actual, singular, or specific events); the unity of method, however, can still be preserved, Popper seems to think, because the historian uses the theories and universal laws of the theoretical sciences of society such as sociology in explaining singular historical events: "a singular event is the cause of another singular event—which is its effect—only relative to some universal laws."[69] But he then qualifies this claim in turn in two important respects. He insists upon the triviality of the laws and theories the historian uses in explaining singular events; and he proceeds to argue that while the approaches or points of view historians use are sometimes "taken for theories" and may actually contain ideas that can be formulated as testable hypotheses this is usually not the case: "those rare ideas inherent in these approaches which can be formulated in the form of *testable hypotheses,* whether singular or universal, may well be treated as scientific hypotheses. But, as a rule, these historical 'approaches' or 'points of view' *cannot be tested.* They cannot be refuted, and apparent confirmations are therefore [?] of no value, even if they are as numerous as the stars in the sky. We shall call such a selective point of view or focus of historical interest, if it cannot be formulated as a testable hypothesis, a *historical interpretation.*"[70]

69. Ibid., 145.
70. Ibid., 150–151. This is the first place we encounter Popper's technical or stipulative use of the word 'interpretation.' Earlier he had used the word in quite a different sense and, in discussing the problem of interpreting different attitudes which prevail in strange social condi-

At this point it seems fair to ask, what has happened to the hypothetical-deductive method, or more precisely, how can the unity of method be regarded as a significant philosophical claim at least where the study of history is concerned? If the laws used in historical explanation are trivial, does this not in effect trivialize the claim that history, although not a theoretical science, does nevertheless employ the hypothetical-deductive method? And if the historical interpretations historians usually employ cannot be *tested* at all, do we not have in effect more of a difference between the methods of history and those of the natural sciences (and the social sciences)? And doesn't this bring Popper in effect into some kind of significant agreement with the anti-naturalistic historicist who has maintained all along that the methods of history are not hypothetical and deductive, do not in other words employ deductive causal explanations such as are found in the natural sciences? Of course, the anti-naturalist wants to claim more than this, for example, that the social sciences are historical and must employ the methods of history and not those of the natural sciences; presumably the anti-naturalist would argue that once Popper grants that the methods of history are not

tions, he recommended the method of trial and error and specifically "thought experiments" on the part of the historian: "And what in the case of historical interpretation we achieve by thought experiment has been achieved by anthropologists in practical field work" (ibid., 95–96). One trouble with the word 'interpretation' is that it can be used to refer to virtually anything the historian might do; certainly it is sometimes used to refer to *testable* hypotheses. One reason Popper's remarks on interpretations may seem more significant than they actually are is that Popper seems (for example, in his remarks on how one historical interpretation might be preferable to another) to trade, or at least to permit the reader to trade, on the ambiguity of the word 'interpretation' or to slide from 'interpretation' in Popper's technical sense to 'interpretation' in the broader, ordinary sense(s).

those of the natural sciences he is well on the road to acknowledging that the methods of the social sciences are not, at least usually or as a rule, the hypothetical-deductive method either. (And there are other resemblances between Popper and the anti-naturalist, which I shall consider in Chapter 3 when I discuss the possibility of historical laws: here Popper in arguing against the possibility of laws explaining the evolutionary and historical processes employs—substantively, though not by the same name—the very arguments concerning "uniqueness" and "generalizations confined to periods" he had rejected in his criticism of anti-naturalistic historicism.)

In summary, there is at least a tension between Popper's advocacy on the one hand of the unity of method in the natural and social sciences *and* history and on the other hand of the theses that the laws historians use are trivial and that many of the hypotheses they use cannot be tested. And if this tension could be resolved, how *important* is Popper's discovery that the unity of method in the natural and social sciences extends to history if the laws historians use are trivial and their hypotheses are often untestable interpretations? This is one reason I have argued against Popper on the issues of triviality and untestability: it is not that he is altogether wrong, for undoubtedly triviality or untestability obtains or may obtain in some cases, but rather that what he says is *unrepresentative* of what goes on in historical inquiry and would, if correct, separate historical method from the methods of the sciences much more than he seems to realize. The unity of method would, I believe, enjoy at best a hollow victory if the historian's hypotheses (whether singular or universal) were rarely testable and if the testable universal hypotheses (laws or theories) were always or even usually trivial. Of course, it might be pointed out that those specific historical hypotheses which are testable need not be trivial and in some cases this may well be true; however, if a specific hypothesis is a causal hypothesis, then given Popper's covering law model of explanation and his views on causation ("a singular event is the cause of another singular event . . . only relative to some universal laws") such a specific causal hypothesis would apparently be an instance of some universal causal hypothesis or law. As such it will be an instance of either a trivial or an informative universal law, and a specific hypothesis that instantiates a trivial universal law will presumably partake of the triviality of that law, while a specific hypothesis that instantiates an informative or nontrivial law constitutes in effect a threat to Popper's insistence upon the triviality of the laws involved in historical explanation.

There is one section in *The Poverty of Historicism,* "The Institutional Theory of Progress," which I have referred to as part of the progression or development of Popper's concern with the unity of method but which must strike most readers as irrelevant or at least an abrupt departure from what he has been discussing in the immediately preceding sections. Popper begins, "In order to make our considerations less abstract, I shall try in this section to sketch, in very brief outline, a *theory of scientific and industrial progress.*"[71] It is doubtful, however, whether the arguments in this section are any less abstract than the preceding ones, and since Popper does not relate his theory of scientific and industrial progress to the problem of whether history can be considered scientific or whether there can be progress in historical inquiry, this section seems to be a new departure more than a development or application of ideas previously expressed. I think that in terms of both what Popper

71. Ibid., 152.

actually says and what he probably had in mind there is no explicit or intended connection between his institutional theory of scientific and industrial progress and the question of whether history is or can be a (progressive) science; however, I find in Popper's development of this theory an argument which *could* be used to show how, in terms of the institutional characteristics of historical inquiry, history might be regarded as being, if not a science, then like a science in several important respects. Accordingly, I regard this section as one in which Popper, unconsciously, makes partial amends for having taken away too much from the unity of (the hypothetical-deductive) method in history and the sciences and for having failed to give us anything like adequate guidelines for distinguishing meritorious historical interpretations from meretricious ones.

Popper looks upon the history of science as being progressive and revolutionary but in some important respects continuous. In this he differs at once from traditional empiricists and inductivists who regarded science as progressive but nonrevolutionary and continuous and from philosophers such as Thomas Kuhn and Paul Feyerabend, who seem to regard science as being revolutionary but nonprogressive and radically discontinuous. Popper places no stock in induction, in gradual accretions of so-called knowledge, or in Kuhn's "normal science" where within the limits set by a paradigm or currently accepted scientific theory scientists do, according to Kuhn, make a sort of relative progress in applying the paradigm or theory in question. For Popper science advances by great conjectural leaps forward and rigorous efforts to determine as quickly as possible not if these conjectures are true but whether they are false—however, Popper believes that even if a theory t_2 eventually fails we can say that it is "nearer to the truth" than theory t_1, if "it contains t_1 as an approximation in a way that explains the success of t_1," and if "it explains all those cases where t_1 failed at least better than did t_1. (This is a kind of—revolutionary—principle of continuity)."[72] While Popper emphasizes the differences between competing scientific theories and the theory-laden nature of scientific observations and tests, he does not locate the problematic of science, as do Kuhn and Feyerabend, in whether competing scientific theories can be regarded as commensurable, as being theories about the *same* phenomena; instead he regards competing scientific theories as being literally theories about the same phenomena, however such phenomena may be described, and his great conjectural leaps forward take place within a continuing tradition where the emphasis falls upon the publicity and criticism of the results of scientific investigations.

It seems obvious that Popper does not regard his claim that science is progressive as an analytic or necessary truth about the meaning of 'science'; nor would he concede that there is after all one sound historicist law informing us that science progresses absolutely and inevitably toward the truth. I believe, however, that he does tend to think of scientific progress as being, to borrow a phrase from Ernest Nagel, contingently necessary; and I shall try to clarify and defend this interpretation of Popper shortly. Among the social institutions Popper mentions in outlining his "institutional theory of progress" are laboratories, scientific periodicals and books, universities and schools, and ultimately language itself:

> Language is a social institution without which scientific progress is unthinkable, since without it there can be neither science nor a growing and progressive tradition. Writing is a social institu-

72. "Replies to My Critics," *The Philosophy of Karl Popper,* II, 1012. See also "Three Requirements for the Growth of Knowledge" in *Conjectures and Refutations,* 240–248.

tion, and so are the organizations for printing and publishing and all the other institutional instruments of scientific method. Scientific method itself has social aspects. Science, and more especially scientific progress, are the results not of isolated efforts but of the *free competition of thought.* For science needs ever more competition between hypotheses and ever more rigorous tests. And the competing hypotheses need personal representation, as it were: they need advocates, they need a jury, and even a public. This personal representation must be institutionally organized if we wish to ensure that it works. And these institutions have to be paid for, and protected by law. Ultimately, progress depends very largely on political factors; on political institutions that safeguard the freedom of thought: on democracy.[73]

According to Popper, the methodology of science is institutionalized and made public, and the institutional and public aspects of science help to protect the scientific method and contribute to the continuing progress of science. The interesting thing about the above passage, I believe, is how easily the word 'history' could be substituted for or added to 'science'; this is not a trivial discovery because other substitutions such as 'poetry,' 'art,' or 'religion' would not fit nearly so well if they would fit at all. Historians need other historians much as scientists need other scientists: the criticism of historical hypotheses, like the criticism of scientific hypotheses, depends upon a community of trained specialists. Of course, the question to what extent historical hypotheses can be subjected to "rigorous tests" suggests that the analogy I wish to make between the community of historians and the community of scientists might need qualifying. If Popper is correct, many of the explana-

73. *The Poverty of Historicism,* 154–155.

tions historians provide in terms of causal hypotheses are untestable, but he notes that historians are also interested in providing detailed descriptions of specific events,[74] and at least some of these descriptions as well as some of the causal explanations historians use can presumably be tested against the evidence they gather from historical documents and other artifacts. In any event, I believe that we can find in the above quotation some of the conditions upon which the progress of historical inquiry depends, and in view of what Popper says about the importance of democracy as a safeguard of the scientific and critical method, we can also find a partial explanation of why historical inquiry, like science, has progressed so rapidly in the democratic period.

In commenting on what he has done, Popper cautions: "I have just sketched some of the institutional conditions on whose realization scientific and industrial progress depends. Now it is important to realize that most of these conditions cannot be called necessary and that all of them taken together are not sufficient."[75] Plainly they are not sufficient as stated above because, as he adds later, there may be "an epidemic of mysticism," the "right man" may not be attracted to scientific research, and we cannot be sure that "there will be men of imagination who have the knack of inventing new hypotheses."[76] But why would Popper say that *most* of the conditions he has noted cannot be called necessary? He explicitly states that scientific progress is "unthinkable" without language; is his modesty in what he claims for his theory only a way of acknowledging that scientific progress could occur,

74. Ibid., 146–147.
75. Ibid., 156.
76. Ibid., 156–157.

though perhaps more slowly, without items such as the printing press, or does it reflect a more serious worry over appearing to claim too much for some of the other conditions he has noted, especially for the political factor? It is very well to speak of the public nature of scientific inquiry and the importance of competition and criticism in the development and testing of hypotheses, Popper might imagine a critic objecting, but it is profoundly unhistorical to connect the growth of science with democratic political institutions—after all we had science *before* we had democracy.

If this is what is bothering Popper, then it may be useful to recall that a similar difficulty confronted Hegel in the Introduction to his *Lectures on the Philosophy of History* when he tried to argue for an essential connection between the growth of literature and the state, while conceding that we had poetry and even great poetry before the advent of the "state" in his technical sense. Though one can imagine all too vividly Popper's probable reaction to this suggestion, Hegel's attempted solution to his problem represents, I believe, the sort of approach Popper should take in seeking to link science with democracy: Hegel maintained that, while we had poetry before we had the state, what we had were isolated monuments to individual genius rather than a continuing literature reflecting the spirit and aspirations of a people. Actually this sort of argument would work a good deal better, I think, in the case of science than in the case of literature, partly because, regardless of the kind of community we live in, literature is "by its very nature" a rather solitary and even lonely discipline, and partly because literature is far less dependent than science upon expensive artifacts such as we find in today's laboratories. I do not, of course, want to relate science directly to anything at once so vague and parochial sounding as "the spirit and aspirations of a people"—like Popper, I see science as an adventure of humanity—but I do want to deny that it is merely a historical accident that science and democracy have flourished together. While totalitarian societies may seek with some success to encourage the growth of science, it is not cant or propaganda to note how science in totalitarian countries frequently seems largely a technological derivative from the science of more open societies, or to wonder how long a critical scientific method can flourish in containment in a society that represses criticism of itself. In short, I believe that Popper would have been correct if he had argued that some approximation to the ideal of the open society is a necessary condition of scientific progress, at least in the long run. And while it is notoriously difficult to provide a list of necessary and sufficient conditions for any phenomenon, I think he has given us good reasons for believing that scientific progress is contingently necessary in this fairly precise sense: given the presence of the institutional factors he cites (including democratic political institutions), the ability of science to continue to attract able champions and imaginative investigators with the "knack" of inventing new hypotheses (here we should recall Popper's claim that there is no logic of scientific discovery), and the absence of certain cultural variables (such as the triumph of mysticism or the decision, democratically arrived at, that science is too dangerous to be permitted any longer), science will continue to be a progressive enterprise.

Perhaps the above formulation claims more for Popper's institutional theory of scientific progress than Popper himself might find acceptable. He writes that "ultimately, much depends on sheer luck in these matters. For truth is *not mani-*

fest"; and he concludes that the results of his "analysis" can be generalized: "The human or personal factor will remain *the* irrational factor in most, or all, institutional social theories."[77] But while Popper's claim that the truth is not manifest is a useful reminder that truth may elude the most persistent investigators and that some important scientific discoveries have come about in unusual and unexpected ways, I believe that my conception of scientific progress as contingently necessary captures much of what he has in mind when he speaks of luck and that my formulation above does justice to his human or irrational factor. In any case, I find that Popper's theory raises this further, exciting possibility: has Popper, in providing us with (at least) some of the necessary conditions of progress in science, also provided a partial basis for a new substantive philosophy of history that might be able to show that virtually all continuous progress within a society depends upon institutional, and methodological, factors such as the ones he has mentioned? Assuming there is no absolute guarantee of progress in any aspect of man's development, has Popper not given us good reasons for believing that in society, as in science, our best hopes for *continuing* progress lie not in charismatic individuals but in institutional protections of freedom and criticism and an institutional means of correcting social and political policies that have failed to meet the "tests" of practical and moral experience? In Chapter 4 I shall discuss Popper's claim that the results of piecemeal social engineering are open to criticism and hence correction in a way in which the results of holistic and utopian social planning are not.

77. Ibid., 157.

CHAPTER THREE

Does History Exist?

In *The Poverty of Historicism* Popper argues that both historicists and "classical historians" fail in their efforts to be objective. Historicists fail to see that there is a plurality of "historical interpretations" of which theirs is only one, and "classical historians" (presumably those historians committed to the Rankean ideal of presenting historical events as they actually did happen) try to avoid "any selective point of view" (any interpretation) altogether and in so doing defeat their own efforts at objectivity. Popper writes, "The way out of this dilemma, of course, is to be clear about the necessity of adopting a point of view; to state this point of view plainly, and always to remain conscious that it is one among many, and that even if it should amount to a theory it may not be testable."[1] In Chapter 2 I expressed doubts as to whether Popper's way out of this dilemma is adequate or whether we needed to get *into* this dilemma in the first place, but I take it that Popper's concern arises not only from his belief that many historical theories and hypotheses are untestable but from his conviction that both historicists and

1. *The Poverty of Historicism,* 152.

classical historians seek to write a history which *cannot* be written. Historicists seek to write about the whole of history and classical historians aim at a definitive universal history of mankind, but what the historicist achieves is, for example, a history interpreted in terms of the class struggle, and the classical historian usually writes a history of political power.

In *The Open Society and Its Enemies* Popper does two things he did not do in *The Poverty of Historicism:* he seeks to explain the (alleged) fact that many historical theories and hypotheses are untestable in terms of the circularity of evidence and theory, or evidence and hypothesis; and he seeks to explain the (alleged) failure of both historicists and classical historians to achieve their goals in terms of the nonexistence of "history" when history is conceived of in a certain way. It seems obvious that Popper's second attempted explanation is the stronger and hence more interesting one, in that it turns not on the question of how historical evidence is come by or whether new evidence may become available, but on the claim that history conceived of in a certain way does not exist—in which case, of course, the question of evidence could not even arise. I think Popper really wants to say, or in terms of his own argument should say, that here there simply is no applicable "idea of objectivity" because history conceived of in a certain way is not a legitimate object of inquiry.

Popper offers the following justification for his assertion that *"history has no meaning":*

In order to give reasons for this opinion, I must first say something about that 'history' which people have in mind when they ask whether it has meaning. So far, I have myself spoken about 'history' as if it did not need any explanation. That is no longer possible; for I wish to make it clear that *'history' in the sense in which most people speak of it simply does not exist;* and this is at least one reason why I say that it has no meaning.[2]

He then asks, "How do most people use the term 'history'?" While empiricists, including some ordinary language philosophers, often consider this kind of question decisive, this is, I believe, the only occasion when Popper raises the question of how people come to use a certain word or concept. He does so here apparently because he sees in the answer to this question an explanation of why people entertain what he considers false beliefs about history (the past) and its relation to the histories they read:

How do most people come to use the term 'history'? (I mean 'history' in the sense in which we say of a book that it is *about* the history of Europe—not in the sense in which we say it *is* a history of Europe.) They learn about it in school and at the University. They read books about it. They see what is treated in the books under the name 'history of the world' or 'the history of mankind', and they get used to looking upon it as a more or less definite series of facts. And these facts constitute, they believe, the history of mankind.

But we have already seen that the realm of facts is infinitely rich, and that there must be selection. According to our interests, we could, for instance, write about the history of art; or of language; or of feeding habits; or of typhus fever. . . . Certainly, none of these things is the history of mankind (nor all of them taken together).[3]

People speak of the history of mankind, but what they have in mind, according to Popper, and what they learned about in

2. *The Open Society and Its Enemies,* II, 269.
3. Ibid., 269–270.

school is the history of political power. (Evidently the texts they used in schools or universities were written by classical historians.) Popper continues:

There is no history of mankind, there is only an indefinite number of histories of all kinds of aspects of human life. And one of these is the history of political power. This is elevated into the history of the world. But this, I hold, is an offence against every decent conception of mankind. It is hardly better than to treat the history of embezzlement or of robbery or of poisoning as the history of mankind. For *the history of power politics is nothing but the history of international crime and mass murder* (including, it is true, some of the attempts to suppress them). This history is taught in schools, and some of the greatest criminals are extolled as its heroes.

But is there really no such thing as a universal history in the sense of a concrete history of mankind? There can be none. This must be the reply of every humanitarian, I believe, and especially that of every Christian. A concrete history of mankind, if there were any, would have to be the history of all men. It would have to be the history of all human hopes, struggles, and sufferings. For there is no one man more important than any other. Clearly, this concrete history cannot be written. We must make abstractions, we must neglect, select. But with this we arrive at the many histories; and among them at that history of international crime and mass murder which has been advertised as the history of mankind.[4]

I find the above passage eloquent and morally appealing, but unconvincing on a number of points. While I believe there is at least one historical law, namely 'Other things being equal, power tends to corrupt,' Popper's reductionist claim that the history of power politics is nothing but the history of inter-

4. Ibid., 270.

national crime and mass murder, while understandable in the historical context in which he wrote *The Open Society and Its Enemies,* seems overstated. And if people tend to think of history in terms of power, and world history in terms of power politics, this is not simply because of what they were taught in school or because of what Popper later describes as an idolatry of power born of fear. As Popper himself notes, one reason why the history of power is selected rather than the history of poetry is that "power affects us all, and poetry only a few."[5] A charitable but not inaccurate account of why "classical historians" have emphasized power and power politics would, I think, acknowledge that these historians believed that power not only affects us all but that the structuring or organization of our lives in political communities, which frequently vie with one another, justifies our writing histories that are mainly political. Of course, humanitarians and Christians might still demand that historians should attend to the meek at least as much as they have previously attended to the powerful, but such demands often reflect moral or religious beliefs that are in a sense extrahistorical and hence not a direct counter to the classical historian's claim that history is best understood in terms of power and power politics.

Suppose, however, that a humanitarian argued not merely that the meek are as morally deserving of consideration as the powerful, but that classical historians have actually exaggerated or distorted the causal significance of the politically powerful in the shaping of historical events. This claim would be a direct challenge to the classical historian's explanations of historical phenomena, and it obviously presupposes that there is something to make exaggerations or distortions about, namely,

5. Ibid.

the past. Does Popper's thesis that history does not exist affect the autonomy or independent existence of the past? I am certain that Popper's claim is not intended as a denial of the common-sense belief in the reality of the past, that is, that certain events have actually occurred at certain times in the past. (I am also certain that his argument is not directed against the rather ethereal doctrine, which so far as I can tell goes unnoticed by Popper, that an event once it has happened continues to exist in some timeless, eternal sense.) What then does Popper wish to deny when he maintains that history does not exist? Evidently he wishes to deny that history consists of "a more or less definite series of facts" and that "these facts constitute . . . the history of mankind." Because history (the past) does not consist of a more or less definite series of facts (in the sense of events), Popper maintains that no definitive history of mankind (no definitive collection of true statements about the history of mankind) can be written. Because "the realm of facts" (events) is "infinitely rich," there must be selection in what we write about. The classical historian has selected political power as his topic, but there are many other topics, ranging from the history of art to the history of typhus fever. I believe that what Popper ultimately wishes to deny is that history or the history of mankind or universal history conceived of as a certain kind of whole can exist or can be considered a legitimate object of inquiry, and to clarify and support this interpretation of Popper I shall now examine what he has to say about "wholes" in *The Poverty of Historicism.* Although Popper himself does not explicitly connect his discussion of wholes to his claims in *The Open Society and Its Enemies* that history does not exist and that history has no meaning, I believe that these claims are not fully intelligible apart from what Popper has said about wholes in *The Poverty of Historicism.*

Popper's claim that history does not exist should, I believe, be regarded as an ontological expression—or corruption—of his epistemological doctrine that "it is not possible for us to observe or to describe a whole piece of the world, or a whole piece of nature; in fact, not even the smallest whole piece may be so described, since all description is necessarily selective."[6] Seen in this light Popper's claim that history does not exist tells us nothing distinctive about history, but rather puts history on a par with other wholes; neither history conceived of as a whole (the entire past of mankind) nor any single historical event (no matter how small) when conceived of as a whole can be said to "exist." Of course, strictly speaking, the most that Popper's thesis that description like all inquiry is necessarily selective could possibly yield in the present connection would be that we cannot know whether or not history taken as a whole exists: to deny (or to affirm) the existence of history taken as a whole would require our being able to go beyond the limits of inquiry Popper himself has pointed out.

In a footnote Popper observes that "the clamour for 'wholes' is a part of mysticism,"[7] and undoubtedly this is often the case. In the text of *The Poverty of Historicism,* however, he acknowledges that there is one respect in which an interest in wholes may be justified (scientifically). There is, he points out, an "ambiguity" in the word 'whole'; it can be "used to denote (a) the totality of all the properties or aspects of a thing, and especially of all the relations holding between its constituent parts, and (b) certain special properties or aspects

6. *The Poverty of Historicism,* 77.
7. Ibid., 78.

of the thing in question, namely those which make it an organized structure rather than a 'mere heap'."[8] Wholes in sense (b) can be and actually have been legitimate objects of scientific inquiry, according to Popper, and he cites the work done by Gestalt psychologists; it is wholes in sense (a) which Popper fervently, and in my judgment rightly, believes can never be legitimate objects of inquiry. And Popper assumes that it is wholes in sense (a) which have been mistakenly regarded as legitimate objects of inquiry, both by classical historians and by historicists.

It is difficult to answer the question whether, as Popper believes, a significant and influential number of thinkers, including not only classical historians and historicists but also political philosophers, social scientists, and social planners, have been "holists" in believing that wholes in Popper's sense (a) can be legitimate objects of scientific inquiry or social planning and control. I find that the quotations Popper gives in support of his assertion that this is so are often ambiguous as to whether their authors actually have in mind wholes in Popper's sense (a) or in his sense (b). I have argued elsewhere that Hegel who, according to Popper, was a thoroughgoing historicist and who certainly did claim to know "the whole of history" was not interested in discovering the totality of all the properties or aspects of history or all the relations holding between its constituent parts; instead Hegel sought to locate those special properties or aspects of history which make the historical process an organized structure rather than a mere heap of events. The structure Hegel believed he had discovered was a teleological one which, he thought, justified his claim

8. Ibid., 76.

that history is essentially though not entirely the story of freedom.[9]

Still, I suppose someone might have said, or might someday propose, that wholes in Popper's sense (a) should be studied or controlled, but this need not be absurd or sinister in *all* the ways that Popper tries to make out. Where wholes in Popper's sense (a) are concerned, I agree with Popper that the "holistic method necessarily remains a mere programme."[10] But programs need not be feasible in order to avoid being pointless, since "ought" does not always imply "can." When the grandmother in one of Isaac Babel's stories says, "You must know *everything*," she isn't implying that her grandson (or anyone) can know everything; and there is some doubt as to whether Jesus expected people to become perfect even if they heeded his counsels of perfection. The point of such counsels is that by trying to do the impossible we may achieve much more than if we had not tried. Counsels such as "Write a definitive history of the whole of mankind or the whole of some particular society or period" may result in more comprehensive and richer histories than would the (in my judgment) more realistic counsel, "Be selective and write the history that interests you." Where the issue of social planning is concerned, although we should always be alert to the totalitarian dangers inherent in what Popper calls "Utopian" or "holistic planning," it is at least arguable that in emergency situations such as war or economic depression such planning may be preferable at least temporarily to efforts to mark the limits of power and to proceed in a "piecemeal" manner. In any case, it is not always

9. See my *Hegel's Philosophy of History* (Ithaca, N.Y., 1974), especially 171–177.
10. *The Poverty of Historicism,* 79.

clear exactly what the difference between holism and Popper's piecemeal social planning amounts to since Popper himself writes that "the difference between Utopian and piecemeal engineering turns out, *in practice,* to be a difference *not so much in scale and scope* as in caution and in preparedness for unavoidable surprises."[11]

Leaving aside the possible heuristic value of proposals that we should seek to know or to control wholes in Popper's sense (a), I think it reasonably clear that there need be no incompatibility between the claim that description and all inquiry is necessarily selective and the claim that we should study wholes in Popper's sense (b). I also believe that if we attend, more carefully than Popper himself does, to the *importance* of the distinction between two senses of the word 'whole,' we can find a way of resolving the controversy over whether historians should study wholes: a division that seems basic and persistent can be shown to be more verbal than substantive. Michael Oakeshott, in considering Lord Acton's recommendation that historians should study problems instead of periods, argues that "there is no difference; a period in the hands of the historian is as much a problem as anything else." Periods, according to Oakeshott, are "beyond question historical individuals," but he concedes that "ideally, I suppose, the subject of a history is not so much a 'period' as a society or social whole."[12] I fail to see the significance of Oakeshott's distinction between a period and a society or social whole—once Acton's distinction between periods and problems is rejected, periods and social wholes would seem to stand on equal

11. Ibid., 69, my italics.

12. "Historical Continuity and Causal Analysis," in *Philosophical Analysis and History,* ed. William Dray (New York, 1966), 211–212.

footing, both being "historical individuals" in Oakeshott's terminology. By way of contrast, J. A. Passmore argues, in a Popperian vein, that "Historians write books . . . with what seem to me to be preposterous titles—titles like *The History of England*. . . . The fact of the matter is that there is no such subject as *The History of England:* a book which purports to be a history of England is either a collection of fragments . . . or else it tacitly confines itself to a more specific problem, say to the changes which have taken place in the distribution of sovereignty."[13] Passmore sees in selectivity a step toward genuine objectivity: once we recognize that no historian can possibly discuss *everything,* we can no longer cite a historian's failure to discuss certain events or aspects of the past as necessarily being evidence of subjectivity or bias on his part. I tend to side with Passmore, Popper, and Lord Acton to the extent of believing that historical inquiry is necessarily selective and also that it is, or should be, a problem-solving enterprise, but I believe that the controversy over whether the description and explanation of social wholes is to count as a legitimate problem for historical investigation need not continue. Two criticisms of Passmore should be noted here: it seems obvious enough that there *is* the history of England where the words 'the history of England' refer to all the events that have occurred in the past of a nation called England; and from the admission (on whatever grounds) that no single history or conjunction of such histories can narrate or explain all of these events it is much too quick to conclude that all efforts to write a book called *The History of England* are preposterous. Such a conclusion could be justified only if we

13. "The Objectivity of History," in *Philosophical Analysis and History,* 84–85.

were to think of the history of England as a whole or totality in Popper's sense (a) and never as a whole in his sense (b). Passmore seems to be saying that it is the impossibility of our writing definitive histories of wholes or totalities in Popper's sense (a) which condemns *all* efforts to write histories of wholes to being either "a collection of fragments" or histories of "some more specific problem" such as the distribution of sovereignty. Oakeshott, however, can be read as a reminder that nothing Passmore, Popper, or Lord Acton has said undercuts the legitimacy of our studying periods or societies as wholes in Popper's sense (b) where we are looking, in Popper's words, for "certain properties or aspects of the thing in question, namely those which make it an organized structure rather than a 'mere heap'." It may be false but it is not obviously absurd to say, using Passmore's example, that the distribution of sovereignty in English history is causally responsible for the history of England's having the structure or form it has and that, moreover, a *History of England* organized around the problem of the distribution of sovereignty will illuminate more aspects, or properties, or events of English history than any other single approach.

I believe that classical historians and historicists, instead of being united, as Popper appears to believe, in a quest for the impossible, namely, the writing of histories of wholes or totalities in Popper's sense (a), tend instead to be united in seeking to write the history of wholes in the structural sense (b), although they are often divided over which factors account for the basic structuring of the period or society under consideration. Classical historians usually emphasize the importance of political institutions, and historicists insofar as they are Marxists or influenced by Marxism are inclined to emphasize the importance of economic factors. Debates between them are often couched in terms of metaphors ('structure' as opposed to 'superstructure,' and so on) and words like 'important' or 'basic' may be used loosely, but the chief intention of both parties seems reasonably clear, namely, to provide an explanation of why a period or society exhibits the characteristics or behavior it does rather than some other characteristics or behavior. It may be that the "weighting" of various causal factors in terms of their relative importance is extremely difficult,[14] but this, I think, is not sufficient reason to conclude either that such a weighting is necessarily arbitrary or subjective as Anatole France and other skeptics have done, or that such a weighting even when done in a judicious, responsible manner could not help to elevate the writing of the history of whole periods or whole societies to the respectable status of a selective, problem-solving activity, as Passmore and Popper seem in effect to believe. In summary, I think that debates between classical historians and historicists as to the relative importance of various factors in determining the structure of a period or society usually involve substantive issues, whereas the questions of whether social wholes, periods, or societies, can be studied seems to me largely a pseudo-issue once we attend seriously to Popper's own distinction between two senses of 'whole.'

The question we must proceed to ask is this: once we grant Popper that no wholes in his sense (a) can be known and that history (the past) taken as a whole or totality in his sense (a) cannot be known, should the history of mankind (the past) be regarded as a "mere heap," *or* as a heap that nevertheless

14. See Ernest Nagel's *The Structure of Science* (New York, 1961), 582–588, for a useful discussion of six senses of 'more important.'

contains various wholes in Popper's sense (b) such as individual persons, periods, and societies; *or* might the history of mankind itself be regarded as a whole in Popper's sense (b), a whole that possesses "certain special properties or aspects . . . which make it appear an organized structure rather than a 'mere heap' "? I shall try first to indicate how I think Popper would respond to this question as I have phrased it, and in this connection I shall comment briefly upon his "methodological individualism" and upon his distinction between mere heaps and structural wholes. I think that it is safe to assume that Popper would want to deny either that the history of mankind is a mere heap or that it can be taken as a whole even in the structural sense (Popper's sense (b)). I take this to be a philosophically significant response: on the one hand, it separates Popper from philosophers and historians who emphasize the role of chance or accident in history and who stress the "uniqueness" of historical events in such a way as to block the recognition of virtually any significant patterns, parallels, or repetitions in the historical process; on the other hand, it separates Popper from teleological historicists (Hegel?), mechanistic historicists (Marx?), and evolutionary historicists who believe that we can find the historical equivalent of the law of biological evolution.

If Popper would accept, as I believe he would, the "middle" position that the history of mankind is neither simply an unstructured heap nor a structured whole, but that it is a heap which nevertheless contains some structured wholes, what exactly would this commit him to? He would, I think, be committed to accepting the claim that we can find individuals, periods, and societies that are structured or organized in certain ways, and that they are structured or organized in the ways they are by virtue of certain properties they possess. And I think Popper does as a matter of fact believe just this, although that he does so may at times be obscured by certain qualifications he wishes to emphasize. First, he is an "anti-essentialist," which here means that he would reject explanations of the structures in question in terms of any *essential* or *defining* properties they might be said to possess.[15] Second, Popper accepts what he calls "methodological individualism," which he wishes to distinguish from any form of "psychologism" or any attempt to explain all of human behavior in terms of psychological laws. His methodological individualism does, however, commit him to a reductionism that insists there can be no behavior or actions of societies, social classes, and institutions which cannot be reduced to the behavior or actions of the individual persons who comprise these societies, classes, and institutions.[16] Third, and finally, Popper would, I think,

15. See the discussion of essentialism versus nominalism in *The Poverty of Historicism,* 26–34. But see my footnote 89 in Chapter 4.

16. See chap. 14 of *The Open Society and Its Enemies,* II, especially 91. One way of describing Popper's methodological individualism would be to say that it insists that only individual persons can be treated as "concrete": Popper is emphatic in rejecting the claim (which he attributes to Troeltsch and Mannheim) that history deals with "concrete individual wholes" which may be persons, events, or epochs. See *The Poverty of Historicism,* 80–81, and *The Open Society and Its Enemies,* II, 270, where he also rejects the possibility of our being able to write a "concrete" history of mankind.

Joseph Agassi, in two suggestive articles, "Methodological Individualism," *British Journal of Sociology,* 11 (1960), 244–270, and "Institutional Individualism," *British Journal of Sociology,* 26 (1975), 144–155, shows how Popper's methodological individualism can avoid some of the limitations of both psychologism and holism. Agassi regards what he terms "institutional individualism" as the most adequate expression of Popper's situational logic, and I believe this is so regardless of whether one conceives of situational logic as explanatory (as Popper and Agassi do) or as evaluative (as I do). In any case, while Agassi does not explicitly discuss the issue of reductionism, his in-

qualify his acceptance of the claim that we can find in the great heap of historical events some structured wholes (individuals, periods, and societies) by raising some doubts about the significance, as contrasted to the validity, of the heap-whole distinction. It was Popper who in describing his second

---

stitutional individualism concedes that institutions exist, though not in the sense that individual persons exist, and that institutions form part of the "circumstances" in which individual persons act; but institutional individualism denies that social wholes or institutions have "distinct aims or interests of their own" and that society, rather than the individual, is "primary." While I am in substantial agreement with Agassi's position, the admission that institutions "exist" needs spelling out: if institutions do not exist in the sense in which individual persons exist, do they exist in any sense other than that in which rules, traditions, and other norms of behavior "exist"? As Agassi points out, much of the importance of methodological individualism lies in its attempt to bypass the question of what there is in the world (ontology) and to focus upon the theory of the study of whatever there is in the world (methodology), but the ontological issue reappears in the insistence by J. W. N. Watkins and others that a "rock bottom" explanation of social phenomena will always be in terms of the behavior of individual agents. I do not propose to explore the problems raised by methodological individualism in this study, but the following remarks may be ventured. Psychologism seems deficient because general observations concerning uniformities of human nature, even if valid, seem unable to explain the varieties of human conduct without mention of institutions; holism, on the other hand, seems unable to provide an explanation of the importance of institutions without "reifying" them in various ways, for example, by insisting that they have aims and interests distinct from those of individual persons. Here, I believe, Popper's insistence upon the importance of the unintended consequences of intentional human behavior may be helpful: perhaps one reason for the belief that institutions have a life of their own is that the actions of persons in institutional contexts, and in following the rules of various institutions, may have results not intended by these persons or sanctioned, implicitly or explicitly, by the rules under which such institutions function. For example, no bureaucrat or social planner may intend that bureaucracy be impersonal and inflexible, but this is usually, if not always, a consequence of bureaucracy; hence the temptation to say that bureaucracies have distinct aims and interests of their own. See also my footnote 20, this chapter.

sense of 'whole' invoked the distinction between "organized structure" and "mere heap"; he then proceeded to say that wholes in this second sense, sense (b), have been made the objects of scientific inquiry, especially in Gestalt psychology. However, at the conclusion of this section (Section 23) Popper writes, "Without retracting anything I have said, I must point out that the triviality as well as the vagueness of the statement that the whole is more than the sum of its parts seems to be seldom realized. Even three apples on a plate are more than 'a mere sum', in so far as there must be certain relations between them (the biggest may or may not lie between the others, etc.): relations which do not follow from the fact that there are three apples, and which can be studied scientifically."[17] Without acknowledging it, Popper has here put his finger on the biggest obstacle confronting his methodological individualism: it is the "reality" of the various relations among individuals that makes the reduction of social wholes to individuals so problematic. While the bare statement that the whole is more than the sum of its parts is trivial, as Popper alleges, this is no guarantee that the spelling out of the ways in which some actual whole is more than the sum of its particular parts will be trivial, and when we shift from Popper's example of three apples to persons, we can expect to encounter rather quickly examples of nontrivial relations—imagine a whole consisting of three individuals, one of whom is more powerful than the other two by virtue of his political or economic position within the group.

Popper continues to press his charge of triviality where "wholes" in his sense (b) are concerned in the following passage:

17. *The Poverty of Historicism,* 82.

What most of the *Gestalt* theorists apparently wish to assert is the existence of two kinds of things, 'heaps', in which we cannot discern any order, and 'wholes', in which an order or symmetry or a regularity or a system or a structural plan may be found. Thus, a sentence such as 'Organisms are wholes' reduces itself to the triviality that, in an organism, we can discern some order. Besides, a so-called 'heap', as a rule, has a *Gestalt* aspect too, just as much as the often cited example of the electrical field. (Consider the regular manner in which pressure increases within a heap of stones.) Thus the distinction is not only trivial, but exceedingly vague; and is not applicable to different kinds of things, but merely to different aspects of the same things.[18]

I believe that Popper's claim that history or "history" does not exist loses much of its strangeness, or initial air of paradox, when it is read as 'The past taken as a whole or totality does not exist' or, better still, as 'There is a sense in which the whole of the past cannot be a legitimate object of historical inquiry or knowledge.' I have tried to specify the sense in which this is true. Inquiry is necessarily selective, and we cannot, according to Popper, know any whole completely; thus, the definitive history of mankind (the whole truth, as it were) cannot be written. I have also considered the question whether the past or any portions of it can be taken as structured wholes in Popper's sense (b), and I have argued that while Popper would reject the claim that the past could be taken as a whole in his sense (b), he would concede that the past "contains" structured wholes such as societies which do constitute legitimate objects of inquiry. However, on close inspection Popper's concession that wholes in his sense (b) may be legitimate objects of inquiry seems a reluctant one. While technically

18. Ibid., 83.

he may be correct in denying that he is retracting anything of what he has previously said, his charges of vagueness and triviality concerning the heap-whole distinction now makes the fruitfulness of any inquiry into wholes in his sense (b) seem doubtful. Heaps no less than wholes may have a *Gestalt* aspect, and this may be true, for example, even of heaps of stones. I suppose that *Gestalt* psychologists and other students of social wholes might attempt to argue for some difference in kind between the *Gestalt* of stones and the *Gestalt* of human psychology, perhaps by appealing in some way to the classic distinction between passive and active phenomena; but Popper has already in effect rejected any such argument in his assertion that the heap-whole distinction is *"not applicable to different kinds of things, but merely to different aspects of the same things"* (my italics). I believe that there are two respects in which what Popper says here is true and one in which it is doubtful, but that the total effect of what he is saying undercuts the significance of some of the things he himself has previously said about the objects of historical inquiry and the limits of historical knowledge. The two respects in which Popper's claim about the heap-whole distinction is true are these: (1) the things in the world are not given to us as heaps or wholes, and the Myth of the Given is as inapplicable here as elsewhere; (2) one and the very same thing may have the properties or aspects of heapness and wholeness—thus, a pile of stones may exhibit heapness where electrical charge is concerned but may exhibit wholeness where regularity of pressure increase is concerned. However, Popper's claim seems doubtful in those cases where inquiry seeks to decide whether an object is more of a structured whole or more of a heap; here an ultimate incompatibility of ascriptions of both heapness and wholeness might emerge. While one might say that nothing or virtually nothing could be a mere heap in all respects, one might nevertheless decide that, comparatively speaking, piles of stones would be ranked below individual persons and individual persons below societies on scales concerned with the number and complexity of structures which things or "piles" of things exhibit.

Popper's points about the vagueness and triviality of ascriptions of wholeness affect, obviously, not only the fruitfulness and significance of inquiries in *Gestalt* psychology but also historicist claims about the various objects of historical inquiry, as such claims are frequently expressed in the language of 'wholes,' 'parts,' 'structures,' and so on. The charge Popper makes concerning the vagueness of the heap-whole distinction is, however, not as damaging as he seems to believe: when he writes that it is applicable not to different things but rather to different aspects of the same thing, he in effect admits that the distinction is not so vague as to be totally inapplicable or useless. Accordingly, I shall concentrate entirely upon his charge of triviality. If, as Popper alleges, the affirmation that something is a whole in his sense (b) is (frequently or usually) trivial,[19] then so, too, is its denial; and this has a direct bearing upon the "debate" between Popper and historicists. Even if all the claims about historical and social wholes in Popper's sense (b) which historicists have advanced thus far were trivial, this would not show that all claims of this sort were necessarily trivial—here Popper seems to fall into much the

19. I have inserted the words 'frequently or usually' in parentheses since Popper writes that atomic physics "studies particle *systems* from a point of view most definitely concerned with wholes in sense (b)" (ibid., 82). Presumably he regards what atomic physics has to say about particle systems, including the claim that they are structured wholes, as nontrivial.

same difficulty as he did when he alleged that the universal laws used by historians to explain particular events are trivial.

More seriously, if, as Popper believes, 'heapness' and 'wholeness' are not applicable to different kinds of things but to different aspects of the same things, if in other words there are no "natural kinds" such that things fall naturally into one of two mutually exclusive categories, then the question of whether history or any portion thereof is a heap or a whole must give way to the question of in what respects history or some portion thereof is a heap and in what respects history or some portion thereof is a whole. Another way of putting this is that questions about whether history or some portion of history is a whole must be answered by investigations into its "properties" or "structures" and not by the assertion that history or some portion of it is just not the kind of thing that could possibly be a whole in Popper's sense (b).

I do not know to what extent, if any, Popper might disagree with what I have said above, but I am certain he would take exception to the two corollaries I shall now propose. (1) If history or some portion of history could be said to possess wholeness in Popper's sense (b), then to speak of history or some portion of history as an "individual" or "historical individual" (as Oakeshott and others sometimes do) is to employ an essentially harmless metaphor.[20] Such a way of speaking

20. For an example of a fruitful use of this metaphor, see A. C. Danto's "The Historical Individual," in *Philosophical Analysis and History,* 266, where Danto distinguishes between "individual human beings" and "social individuals": "Examples of social individuals might be social classes (the German bourgeoisie in 1618), national groups (the Bavarians), religious organizations (the Protestant Church), large-scale events (the Thirty Years War), large-scale social movements (the Counter-Reformation), etc." I am persuaded mainly by Clifton B. Perry that the controversy between methodological individualists and holists turns on the question of whether social individuals can be causally efficacious.

need only indicate the presence of some property or aspect which makes societies, for example, resemble individual persons to the extent of being legitimate objects of inquiry; it does not necessarily prejudge the question whether the actions of these "individuals" are reducible to the actions of individual persons. (2) The assertion that history or some portion of history is a whole by virtue of its having certain properties which make it appear an organized structure is, when taken by itself, entirely compatible with the claim that it has properties which give it moral meaning or significance, and indeed with the claim that the properties which make it appear an organized structure are the very same properties which give it moral meaning or significance. A *separate argument* would be required to show either that it does not have such properties or that such properties cannot give it moral meaning or significance. Such an argument is to be found, as I shall attempt to show in the next chapter, in Popper's dualism between facts and moral values, but no argument to the effect that history or the portion of history in question is a heap of events ("one emergency following another," as H. A. L. Fisher remarked in his *History of Europe* in a passage quoted approvingly by Popper)[21] would by itself undercut either the claim that history or the portion of history in question is also a structured whole or the further claim that it is a structured whole which has moral meaning. By the logic of Popper's own remarks on the heap-whole distinction, the claim that history or some portion of history is a structured whole and the claim that it is a heap are, to a point at least, compatible positions. (The compatibility in question differs from the alleged compatibility of "points of view" discussed in the previous chapter: although

21. *The Poverty of Historicism*, 109.

the two claims involve different ways of looking at the "same phenomena," the question whether history or some portion of history has a certain structure should be seen as an empirical matter, which, in Popperian terms, means that the claim that history or some portion of it has a certain structure should be regarded as falsifiable. The point at which the claim that history or some portion of it is a structured whole and the claim that it is a heap might become incompatible is reached, as I noted earlier, when we want to know whether history or some portion of it is more of a structured whole or more of a heap.) Also, the claim that history or some portion of history is a structured whole which possesses moral meaning and the claim that it is an unstructured heap which does not possess moral meaning are, to a point at least, compatible positions. (The point at which these claims might become incompatible is reached when we want to know whether history or some portion of it has more moral meaning or more "meaninglessness"—if Popper and I are correct, this is not, of course, an empirical matter or question of fact.)

Why has Popper failed to see that his claim that " 'history' . . . does not exist" is *not* "at least one reason" for saying that history has no meaning?[22] Briefly I want to suggest that Popper has mistakenly assumed that history can have no moral meaning *because* it cannot be known as a whole or totality in his sense (a) when actually all that would be required in this connection to show that history could have moral meaning or significance would be to show that history could be a structured whole in his sense (b). Popper, apparently without realizing the implications of his claim that the heap-whole distinction is not applicable to different kinds of things but

22. See *The Open Society and Its Enemies,* II, 269.

rather to different aspects of the same things, has given us reason to reject at least one argument—the argument from "natural kinds"—which purports to show that history just isn't the kind of thing that can be a structured whole. 'History does not exist' if it were taken to mean that history does not exist as a structured whole could only be taken as a confession that we have not yet found the properties which might make it a structured whole—here we would be in a position comparable to that of the man who has not yet discovered the regularity of pressure increase within a pile of stones. Of course, we might never find those properties which would make history a structured whole, but this could not justify any claim to the effect that history just isn't the kind of thing that could be a structured whole.

I believe that in two important respects Popper's discussion of "wholes" could not support his claim that history does not exist and consequently can have no moral meaning. (1) Popper seems to allow that some portions of history, societies for example, could be structured wholes in his sense (b), and nothing in his remarks about heaps and wholes rules out the possibility that history—and not merely some portions of it—could after all be a structured whole. As a structured whole, history might turn out to be structured in a variety of ways. In other words, history might have a number of different properties resulting in a number of different structures, in which case it might have (at least) as many moral meanings as it has structures. (2) An argument to the effect that history does not exist or cannot be known as a whole or totality in Popper's sense (a) might also suggest that the quest for a single overall moral meaning in history is ill advised. On the assumption, which may be arguable, that any whole in Popper's sense (a) would have only a single structure and thus would have only a single overall moral meaning, the following position might seem reasonable: just as we despair of finding definitiveness or completeness on the "level" of facts so we might also despair of finding definitiveness or completeness where any single overall moral meaning in history is concerned. However, despair over finding a single overall moral meaning in history ("*the* meaning of history," as it is sometimes called) is no reason to despair over history's having a plurality of moral meanings, (at least) as many moral meanings as it has structures. Popper, of course, might find some slight cause for cheer where this point about the plurality of meanings is concerned, but for him such a plurality of meanings could only reflect our various changing needs and concerns and could not be something we discover in or about history or its various structures. With some reluctance I have had to conclude that nothing Popper says about "wholes" could block the historicist who wants to claim that history *does* exist, as a structured whole in Popper's sense (b), and that history has moral meaning or significance as one of its "properties" or "aspects."

In the next chapter I shall discuss the adequacy of Popper's dualism between "facts and standards" as an answer to the historicist who believes that moral meaning is constitutive of the nature of historical reality and that this moral meaning can be read off or inferred from the facts of history, but first I wish to examine some of the implications of Popper's treatment of "wholes," especially as it relates to the claims advanced by evolutionary historicism. In the first chapter I quoted Popper's preliminary definition of historicism as "an approach to the social sciences which assumes that *historical prediction* is their principal aim, and which assumes that this aim is attainable by discovering the 'rhythms' or the 'patterns', the 'laws' or the 'trends' that underlie the evolution of history."[23] I have doubts about the adequacy of this as a general characterization of both pro-naturalistic and anti-naturalistic historicism; significantly Popper's characterization of anti-naturalistic historicism in *The Poverty of Historicism* yields these results: the anti-naturalistic historicist is alleged to believe that he may be "unable to formulate general laws which would serve as a description in general terms" of the causes and effects of any particular events, that even if there were immutable sociological uniformities, they might be too complex for us to discover, and that prediction of social phenomena is necessarily difficult and inexact.[24] This description scarcely supports any reading of the anti-naturalistic historicist as being primarily concerned with social prediction, and if we read Hegel as an anti-naturalistic historicist it is significant to note that he at least did not regard the prediction of social phenomena as being feasible.[25] Since Popper himself regards prediction as at least one of the principal aims of the social sciences, and since furthermore his covering law model commits him to denying any logical asymmetry between prediction and explanation, it may be difficult for the reader to locate the exact differences between Popper and the historicist. Tentatively, I suggest the following: that we see Popper as believing that prediction is a principal goal of the social sciences—here he explicitly admits a resemblance

23. *The Poverty of Historicism,* 3.
24. Ibid., 9–14.
25. See my *Hegel's Philosophy of History,* 72–84.

between himself and the pro-naturalistic historicist,[26] but he goes on to distinguish bona fide prediction from unscientific prophecy and to argue in effect that we cannot discover the 'rhythms,' the 'patterns,' the 'laws,' or the 'trends' which underlie the evolution of history *conceived of as a whole*—here, although he does *not* acknowledge this, some of his reasons for denying that we can find such rhythms, patterns, laws, or trends turn out to be adaptations of arguments which, when he attributed them to the anti-naturalistic historicist, were repudiated by Popper! In other words, Popper can be read as using some of the arguments of the anti-naturalistic historicist to show that the pro-naturalistic historicist's conception of what we can accomplish in the way of "historical prediction" is wildly optimistic and logically deficient.

In *The Poverty of Historicism* Popper denies that there can be a law of evolution for either biological or historical phenomena, and his two principal reasons for this seem to be that the evolution of life, whether biological or social, is "a unique historical process" and that, while a trend or trends may be discerned in such a process, trends ought not to be confused with laws. Popper's supporting argument for these two claims is in keeping with what one would expect in the light of his previous discussion of wholes. On the one hand, he wants to concede that there may be repetitions and parallels among historical phenomena, but on the other hand he wants to deny that the evolution of human society can be subsumed under any law(s) of social or historical evolution. The evolution of human society, according to Popper, proceeds in accordance with all kinds of causal laws, but the "description"

26. *The Poverty of Historicism,* 12–13.

of this process is "not a law but only a singular historical statement." Popper concedes that the observation of one single instance may "incite" us to formulate a universal law which may, if we are lucky, even be true; however, "it is clear that any law, formulated in this or in any other way, must be *tested* by new instances before it can be taken seriously by science."[27]

The claim that there can be no law(s) of social or historical evolution has, of course, been frequently challenged, most notably in our time by Arnold Toynbee's *Study of History,* and Popper attempts to meet this challenge in two ways. First, he argues that, while there are repetitions within the historical process, such repetitions take place under "vastly dissimilar" circumstances, and thus we have "no valid reason to expect of any apparent repetition of a historical development that it will continue to run parallel to its prototype."[28] Second, Popper alleges that Toynbee "classifies as civilizations only such entities as conform to his *a priori* belief in life cycles," and that Toynbee's distinction between primitive societies and civilizations (as being different species of the same genus) is based only on his "*a priori* intuition into the nature of civilizations."[29] The entire question of whether primitive societies and civilizations belong to the same species, Popper asserts, "is inadmissible, for it is based on the scientistic method of treating collectives as if they were physical or biological bodies."[30] The whole of society does not move; there are, Popper maintains, "only changes of selected aspects." Popper writes, "The

27. Ibid., 108–109.
28. Ibid., 111.
29. Ibid.
30. Ibid. Popper borrows the word 'scientistic' from F. A. von Hayek to describe misunderstandings or misuses of the scientific method.

idea of the movement of society itself—the idea that society, like a physical body, can move *as a whole* along a certain path and in a certain direction—is merely a holistic confusion."[31] Popper concedes that there are trends or tendencies in social change, but "*laws and trends are radically different things.*"[32] Statements asserting the existence of a trend are singular and existential; laws by contrast are universal and nonexistential—they do not tell us that something exists but, as Popper puts it, they assert the impossibility of something, for example, that you cannot have full employment without inflation.[33] Scientific predictions can be based upon laws, but they cannot be based merely on the existence of trends, as trends may change, often quite rapidly. Popper acknowledges that trends do exist, although their persistence depends upon certain initial conditions, and he concedes that there may be laws about trends, laws taking the form 'Whenever there are conditions of the kind *c* there will be a trend of the kind *t*'.[34] However, he appears to attach little importance to this concession, probably because of (1) his conviction that historicists have confused conditional trends with unconditional laws (laws may *state* conditions under which phenomena will occur but they are unconditional in the sense of being universally valid) and have mistakenly believed that certain trends are absolute and irreversible, and (2) his earlier claim that there cannot be laws about the unique historical process. In other words, Popper believes that while there may be laws about some trends, there can be no laws about trends which obtain where the historical process taken as a whole is concerned.

31. Ibid., 114.
32. Ibid., 115–116.
33. Ibid., 61–63.
34. Ibid., 128–129.

I shall leave largely unanswered the question of how cogent Popper's criticisms of various "historicists" (in the present connection he seems to have in mind mainly J. S. Mill and Auguste Comte) actually are. I happen to agree that historicists do at times show a lack of imagination where the possibility that certain trends may not persist is concerned, but I am not sure whether this is because they have "confused" trends with laws or because they have overlooked the dependence of trends upon initial conditions. An alternative explanation of their perhaps excessive conviction that certain trends will persist would be in terms of their (perhaps excessive) certainty that the initial conditions upon which these trends depend will continue to obtain. In any case, I am not overly impressed by Popper's claims as to what *cannot* be done where the prediction of the direction of a society or even the entire historical process is concerned. Most of my reservations about this aspect of his argument are implicit in my criticism of his earlier remarks about wholes, and I shall try to be as brief as possible in the application of what I said previously.

Popper's basic assumption, I believe, in arguing against the possibility of there being a law of historical evolution is the correctness of his earlier strictures against "holism." This comes out in a variety of ways, for example, in his condemnation of the historian Henry Adams and the evolutionist C. H. Waddington for speaking of the motion or movement of social bodies or systems, and in his criticism of Toynbee for treating human collectives as if they were physical or biological bodies. What can we do with Popper's claim that "the idea that society, like a physical body, can move *as a whole* along a certain path and in a certain direction—is merely a holistic confusion" except to say that this claim is itself confused, that Popper has confused wholes or totalities in his sense (a) with structured wholes in his sense (b), and that changes in "selected aspects" of a society is *all* that is required in this connection for us to make sense of the idea that a society (or even the entire historical process) conceived of as a structured whole might move in a certain direction? To give a specific example, the continued existence of Mennonite communities in the United States could scarcely count as evidence against the claim that there is in American society a trend or tendency away from individual dependence upon the family and the community. Popper, of course, is right in cautioning us not to bet too heavily on the persistence of any trends; in the present example, the emergence of communes and "extended families" may be evidence of a growing reaction against the phenomenon of individual isolation, and this reaction may lead to a slowing down or reversal of the trend in question. But nothing in this sort of discussion of the direction in which American society is moving need involve any "holistic confusion."

Let us now examine the claim that while there can be laws about some trends, there can be no laws about trends which allegedly pervade the historical process taken as a whole. First, however, we should consider whether it is possible that there could be a law about the trend toward individual independence of or isolation from the family and the community in American society. I suppose Popper would say that there could be, provided (1) we could isolate the causal factor(s) or condition(s)—for example, loss of religious faith or continued industrialization—responsible for this change in the structure of our society,[35] and (2) we could test this law against other

35. In discussing laws about trends, however, Popper expresses doubts as to how we could "determine that our conditions are sufficient" for

instances, in this case other societies where we could determine if the same factor was having similar effects. The difference between cases of this sort and trends that are said to pervade the entire historical process would presumably be, for Popper, that there are many societies and hence repeated opportunities for testing laws about trends such as the one given in my example, while there is only one historical process and hence no additional opportunities for testing laws that allegedly explain trends which are said to pervade the entire historical process. So even if there are general historical trends of this kind, we can only *describe* them; a causal explanation of such trends is beyond our powers. But is this true?

To begin with, are we sure that Popper's criticism of Toynbee's distinction between civilizations and primitive societies doesn't also apply to our example? Presumably in comparing American society to other societies we might omit some

---

the occurrence of a certain kind of trend (ibid. 129), or in other words how we could *test* a law about trends; but neither in this passage nor elsewhere does he give good reasons why this need be any more problematic for historical and social trends than for other phenomena. Also, he denies, with special reference to Auguste Comte, that there can be any laws of historical succession or historical dynamics (if dynamics is properly understood): "But there can be no single law, such as that of gravity, nor even a single definite set of laws, to describe the actual or concrete succession of causally connected events" (ibid., 117). He gives as an example of this problem the wind shaking a tree and Newton's apple falling to the ground. Undoubtedly, we do not have laws, causal or otherwise, relating successive phenomena, physical or social, under *all descriptions* of such phenomena; so far as I know, there is no law of physics about Newton's apple or even about apples as such, but there are laws of physics explaining the effects of wind velocities upon bodies of certain weights and shapes, the pull of gravitational forces, and so on. Popper's discussion of his own example acknowledges this, but what he fails to make clear is why a conjunction (or "definite set") of such laws cannot explain causally connected events or phenomena that occur in a certain succession. What does succession add to our problems besides complexity?

societies, for example, pre-industrial ones, much as Toynbee neglected "primitive societies." Would this be methodologically defensible, or would it depend on some "a priori" or arbitrary intuition about the nature of society? Perhaps we should say here what Popper has said in effect in discussing the heap-whole distinction: social phenomena do not come to us labeled as wholes, but we classify them as wholes provided they possess certain properties that make them structured in some but not all respects. In other words, the question of whether something is actually a society or civilization—or historical process—is open-ended in the sense of awaiting our discovery of whether it possesses properties sufficient to account for its being structured in a certain way. (That Toynbee has an "a priori intuition," or a theory about what a society is should not worry anyone, least of all Popper, who believes that theory is prior to observation and that the source of our theories is in any case irrelevant to the question of their truth.) In speaking of the succession of historical events as "the historical process" we may be suggesting, or allowing, that something besides mere pastness might serve to structure or unite these events in various ways. But suppose there is only one historical process which is so structured: is it true, as Popper in effect alleges, that our discoveries about this process, as contrasted with our discoveries about certain of the events that comprise it, can at best count only as *descriptions* and not as *explanations?*[36] I

36. Popper writes of "the evolution of life on earth or of human society" that it is "a unique historical process": "Such a process, we may assume, proceeds in accordance with all kinds of causal laws, for example, the laws of mechanics, of chemistry, of heredity and segregation, of natural selection, etc. Its description, however, is not a law, but only a singular historical statement" (ibid., 108). Such a singular historical statement would, obviously, have to be a conjunction of many singular historical statements, and whether or not the realm of historical facts

take it that one of the main contributions Popper makes in *The Logic of Scientific Discovery* and elsewhere is to cast doubt upon the epistemological significance of the distinction between observation and theory, and I fail to understand how a distinction between description and explanation (or description and law) could survive as epistemologically viable in the face of such doubts. Assuming, however, that there is still merit in Popper's demand that any law of historical change must not merely redescribe or restate what has occurred but must explain or account for such change, it seems reasonably clear that the claim that certain events constitute a structured whole *because* they possess a certain common property or aspect is offered *as an explanation,* usually of a causal sort. The crucial question then is whether such explanations can be acceptable in lieu of that testing by "new instances" which Popper demands, and this difficulty brings us back once more to the alleged uniqueness of the historical process.

Formally, of course, a statement may be considered a law regardless of how many instances of it we may have. And in fact some laws are considered acceptable even if there is only one instance of the law in question—apparently some of the laws of astronomy are like that. Or a law may be acceptable even when we have no instances of it at all; for example, there could be a law stating that an organism could not survive at an extremely high temperature which at present we are unable to produce. But such laws, Popper might reply, are acceptable only because they are derivations from, or extensions of, other

(events) is "infinitely rich" (infinite in number?), as Popper claims, the list of historical statements we might make about such facts or events would be infinitely long in that our descriptions (and explanations) of events will always be affected by our changing interests in, and theories about, past phenomena.

laws or theories which have been tested, and conceived of in this way such laws serve only to underscore how far we really are from having laws about the unique historical process. Of course, Popper could concede that we might someday discover, on other planets, people or "people" with historical processes sufficiently similar to our own to be usable in the testing of laws about historical processes. The 'cannot' in Popper's claim that we cannot have a law of historical change, like the 'cannot' in his claim that historical interpretations cannot be tested, can be read as a contingent 'cannot'—we cannot on the basis of presently available information decide whether certain statements which may have the form of a law actually are laws or not. However, while it is conceivable that our historical process is not unique, we have at present no reason to suppose it is not and hence no good reason to suppose that any "laws" about it can ever be tested.

The reply I have imagined Popper might make seems, up to a point, highly persuasive; there is, however, at least a tension between his willingness to accept the subsumption of particular historical events under universal laws and his refusal to sanction the subsumption of the historical process under such laws. At times Popper seems to be saying that the historical process just isn't the sort of thing that could be subsumed under universal laws, and in this respect his position resembles the argument from the uniqueness of historical events as used by some opponents of the covering law model. It is interesting to note how, later in *The Poverty of Historicism,* Popper in trying to do justice to "the *uniqueness* of historical events" writes that history "is interested not only in the explanation of specific events but also in the description of a specific event as such. One of its most important tasks is undoubtedly to describe interesting happenings in their peculiarity or uniqueness."[37] Popper has denied that any causal explanation of the historical process can be forthcoming and has insisted that we can only describe this process, in its peculiarity or uniqueness, but at the very end of his discussion of the "uniqueness" of historical events he observes that "at one time an event may be considered typical, i.e. from the standpoint of its causal explanation, and at another time unique."[38] I want to suggest that what is true of an event can be true of a process, or any phenomenon, and that Popper's failure to see the full force of the relativity of ascriptions of uniqueness or typicalness to our standpoint (interest) results in his making too much of the uniqueness of the historical process. Specifically, Popper has failed to appreciate the potential in a method practiced quite commonly, if somewhat primitively, by "speculative" (or substantive) philosophers of history, namely that of "breaking down" the historical process into various subprocesses and then proposing a law or laws which purport to explain these subprocesses and to be generalizable to the historical process conceived of as a (structured) whole. Toynbee's study of civilizations with his Law of Challenge and Response is a putative example of this method. Perhaps Toynbee misused the method and perhaps his "Law" was formulated in such a way that it could not possibly be falsified by negative instances; but, without passing judgment in this particular case, I think it is reasonable to affirm that this method, when properly used, does allow us to find negative instances of laws which purport to explain the evolution of human society *and* that we can do this on the

37. Ibid., 146–147.
38. Ibid., 147.

basis of information already available to us in the form of historical records and artifacts.[39]

Popper's claim that all repetitions in history have occurred under "vastly dissimilar" circumstances and that, therefore, we have "no valid reason to expect of any apparent repetition of a historical development that it will *continue* to run parallel to its prototype"[40] is at best a cautionary remark, and it is potentially misleading given Popper's skepticism about induction. Dissimilar circumstances *per se* are not, I think, a valid reason *not* to expect a repetition of a historical development to continue along certain lines, provided we have located the relevant variables that account for the resemblances between some particular historical development and what Popper calls its "prototype." Here Popper seems to have forgotten his own rejection of the importance the anti-naturalistic historicist attaches to the variability of experimental conditions and of the anti-naturalistic historicist's claim that generalizations about social phenomena must be confined to the period in which they occur and that no (significant) regularities can be detected in different social and historical environments. (The reader should compare pages 93–104 with pages 110–111 of *The Poverty of Historicism.* My own preference is for the

39. Biologists sometimes maintain that a multiplicity of evolutions of different genera may be the basis for generalizations about the evolutionary process. Popper objects that this still will not yield a law of evolution: "But this comparison of evolutions has merely led to the description of *types* of evolution" (ibid., 110–111). Here, as in the case of the evolution of social life, Popper is arguing that we can only describe and not explain, but if we can even describe *types* of biological or social evolution, then the force of the argument from the uniqueness of the process of biological or social evolution is diminished—and it is worth noting that typology has often progressed from mere taxonomy to the formation of complex theories and laws.

40. Ibid., 111.

arguments advanced on pages 93–104, and I especially like Popper's bold claim that "we must allow the experimental method to take care of itself," a point made in connection with the problem of the bearing of any observed difference or similarity upon the possibility of reproducing an experiment, but one which is clearly applicable to the issue of how important an obstacle "vastly dissimilar" circumstances really are where the repetition of historical developments is concerned.)

Whether one believes there can be *any* valid reason to suppose that an apparent repetition of a historical development will *continue* to run parallel to its "prototype" depends, I should think, upon what one construes to be a valid reason for all cases involving expectations about the future, and *not* upon any alleged peculiarities either of the "unique historical process" or of our efforts to find laws which explain this process. It seems fairly obvious that if we reject induction, as Popper does, valid reasons for believing that *any* phenomena will continue to develop along certain lines will be difficult or impossible to come by. If, like Popper, we dismiss apparent confirmations of a law or theory as being of no value,[41] then any "valid reasons" for believing that certain regularities will obtain will turn upon the retrospective judgment that laws or theories informing us that such regularities will persist have not yet been falsified. Popper writes, "Of nearly every theory it may be said that it agrees with many facts: this is

41. Popper writes that, once we believe in a law of repetitive life cycles, "we are sure to discover historical confirmation of it nearly everywhere. But this is merely one of the many instances of metaphysical theories seemingly confirmed by facts—facts which, if examined more closely, turn out to be selected in the light of the very theories they are supposed to test" (ibid., 111). For Popper, however, all "confirmations" of a theory, regardless of how the facts which "support" them are selected, are equally worthless.

one of the reasons why a theory can be said to be corroborated only if we are unable to find refuting facts, rather than if we are able to find supporting facts."[42] Whether corroboration can give us "valid reasons" for expecting certain regularities to obtain and, if so, whether corroboration can still be said to differ significantly from confirmation constitutes one of the most complex and controversial issues in Popper's philosophy of science and epistemology. On the one hand Popper wants to say that all laws and theories are conjectures or guesses and that corroboration is not a *measure* of verisimilitude or truth-likeness, but on the other hand he does believe that we can rationally prefer those theories and laws which have not been falsified over those theories and laws which have been falsified, and that corroboration, while not a measure of verisimilitude, is an *indicator* of verisimilitude.[43] However this problem is resolved (if it admits of resolution), I want to suggest one disquieting similarity between Popper and the historicist where "valid reasons" for expectations about the future are concerned. Since for Popper confirmation is worthless, only corroboration merits attention here. Now either corroboration can or cannot provide anything like "valid reasons" for our having various beliefs about the future and for our thinking that, while all beliefs about the future are conjectural, some are rationally preferable to others. If it cannot, then all beliefs

42. Ibid.

43. *Conjectures and Refutations,* 234–235. "Replies to my Critics," 1011. Wesley Salmon, "Justification of Inductive Rules of Inference," and J. W. N. Watkins, "Non-Inductive Corroboration," *The Problem of Inductive Logic,* ed. Imre Lakatos (Amsterdam, 1967), 24–43 and 61–66. Imre Lakatos, "Popper on Demarcation and Induction" *The Philosophy of Karl Popper,* I, ed. Paul Arthur Schlipp (La Salle, Ill., 1974), 241–273. Gary E. Jones, "Popper and Theory Appraisal," to appear in ***Studies in History and Philosophy of Science.*** See also my footnote 50 in Chapter 4.

about the future, including those held by the historicist, are equally groundless, with the result that the historicist is no worse—or better—off than anyone else, but if corroboration can provide anything approximating "valid reasons" for any of our beliefs about the future, such reasons could only reflect our preference for those laws or theories which have not as yet failed or been falsified. Traditionally it would seem that the historicist has been wedded to induction and the belief that some statements about the future are better confirmed than others; but it is questionable whether, as Popper apparently assumes, historicism stands or falls, logically speaking, with inductivism. At least one can imagine a historicist, shorn of his faith in the value of confirming instances, arguing that he is still no worse off than Popper: just as Popper prefers those laws and theories which have not as yet failed or been falsified so the historicist may do likewise, and where historical *trends* are concerned, the historicist may continue to prefer those trends which have not yet failed to persist.[44]

Since all or virtually all of us believe, on whatever grounds, that some regularities will continue to obtain, that *some* "repetitions" of various developments, whether historical or physical, "will continue to run parallel" to their prototype,[45] I shall

44. In the above formulation I have tried to stay as close as possible to Popper's terminology. According to Popper, no theory is "reliable" (can be shown to be true), but some theories can be "preferred" to others. All theories belong to *"conjectural knowledge,"* he says: "But some conjectures are much better than others, and this is a sufficient answer to Russell, and it is sufficient to avoid radical skepticism. . . . We may *prefer* some competing theories to others on purely rational grounds" ("Replies to My Critics," 1022).

45. Popper concedes there may be after all a "whiff" of inductivism in his position: "It enters with the vague realist assumption that reality, though unknown, is in some respects similar to what science tells us, or, in other words, with the assumption that science can progress towards

in the remainder of this section restrict my discussion to what the historicist says, or might say, about the persistence of certain historical trends. I think Popper would want to raise two objections to what I have done in the above paragraph. First, while he might acknowledge that a historicist could conceivably argue that a certain trend has not yet failed to persist (anyone could do that), in point of fact the historicist talks as if his favorite trend will necessarily persist ("He firmly believes in his favourite trend, and conditions under which it would disappear are to him unthinkable. The poverty of historicism, we might say, is a poverty of imagination").[46] Second, while Popper might agree that, of course, it would be desirable if the historicist said simply that his favorite trend has not yet failed to persist, such a formulation would still not obscure the fundamental difference between scientific laws and historicist talk about trends, namely, that scientific laws invite falsification by telling us that certain things cannot happen, while historicist talk about trends admits only of (worthless) confirmation by new instances. The first "objection" may be persuasive in historical and psychological terms; we all know of cases in which individuals, and not only historicists, have talked as if certain trends would necessarily persist, and it is always useful to be reminded that the "waves of the future" may either be nonexistent or may recede before they engulf us. However, the second response that I have imagined Popper might make seems to me unconvincing, perhaps because of some lingering commitment to induction

---

greater verisimilitude" ("Replies to My Critics," 1193). Science, of course, tells us that certain regularities will, under certain conditions, continue to obtain.

46. *The Poverty of Historicism,* 129–130.

on my part but certainly because of Popper's own concession that there may after all be laws about trends. Once this concession is made, one has admitted in effect that, whatever historicists may actually have said about certain trends as being absolute and irreversible, he can henceforth talk about trends in a more rational manner, can attempt to specify the conditions under which trends of certain kinds will—or will not—obtain. The formulation and testing of laws about trends would, at least in terms of Popper's own argument, involve the comparison of trends with one another. Once any application of what historians and political scientists (and speculative philosophers of history) have sometimes called "the comparative method" is allowed, there can be no metaphysical or methodological reasons—or none that Popper could consistently accept—for excluding any thing or collection of things from subsumption under laws. Whether something is a whole, a process, or even a trend depends upon its properties and structures; and we cannot say in advance of inquiry that the comparative method cannot apply to certain things because these things are by their very nature unique. If this is so, then philosophers of Popper's (and my) general orientation can consistently adopt only a "wait and see" (or wait and test) attitude where the search for laws about wholes, processes, and even trends is concerned.

Despite my criticisms I still find considerable merit in what Popper has said. First, his distinction between two senses of 'whole' can help us distinguish between inquiries that are feasible and those that are not, and this distinction can also be profitably applied to processes and even to trends, since processes and trends may be regarded as species of wholes, or at least very much like wholes in the requisite respects. Second, Popper's reflections on the heap-whole distinction suggest that, since this distinction applies not to different kinds of things but to different aspects of the same things, we might cease worrying about whether or not something is (by its very nature, or essentially) a whole and instead investigate its properties in order to determine in what respects it may be considered a structured whole. Third, Popper's concession that there can be laws about trends narrows the gap between himself and a Reformed Historicist so that instead of continuing, as Popper does, to emphasize the differences between laws and trends, we can get on with the business of subsuming trends under laws. I'm afraid that here I may be emphasizing aspects of Popper's achievement which he might ignore or play down, but I have been looking toward the future. I cannot believe that historicism in some form or other will not persist or recur—the desire or need to predict the future course of various societies or even of the entire historical process is too deeply imbedded in many of us to be eradicated by a thousand *Poverties*. Here I disagree with J. W. N. Watkins's claim that "the holist-historicist position has . . . been irretrievably damaged by Popper's attacks on it."[47] And in any event, my present emphasis has fallen not upon battles Popper has won, but upon how his victories might help to shape some more responsible versions of historicism than we have had thus far.

The three aspects of Popper's achievement noted above constitute a good reason why a future historicist should be less confident about the persistence of any trend than previous

47. "Historical Explanation in the Social Sciences," *British Journal for the Philosophy of Science*, 8 (1957), 108.

historicists have often been. Popper, in his remarks about structured wholes, in his perhaps unintended sanctioning of the quest for the different ways in which wholes or processes might be structured, and in his argument that trends which are not subsumed under laws can have no legitimate predictive function, has, I think, given any open-minded historicist reason to reconsider an excessive reliance upon any trend. Since any thing or any collection of things can be a structured whole, it is conceivable that the same thing or collection of things may be structured in more than one way; and it is also conceivable that something which is a part of one whole may also be a part of another whole or wholes. The historicist may have erred here not in insisting that this particular society or this particular process, or the entire historical process, is a structured whole, but in not seeing sufficiently that it may be structured in many ways, some of which may be compatible with one another but others of which may be incompatible or at odds with one another. (Where the historicist has seen something like this, he has perhaps been too quick in resolving or explaining the incompatibility or tension between various structures by assigning the different structures to different historical stages or periods and by announcing, for example, that some structures, properties, or aspects, of a society or a period are "recessive" or "residual"—this may work in some cases, but it is no general solution for the problem at hand.)

Since in the next chapter I shall consider Popper's arguments against historicism conceived of as a moral philosophy, I want to suggest here that the historicist's moral certainty might be shaken somewhat by the realization that the whole, the process, or trend which he is so confident will prevail, and which he is often so uncritical of, may contain many—sometimes incompatible—structures. The argument from the complexity of the world or its various parts is notorious for corrupting overly simple moral or religious faiths, and I wish the argument from complexity would start earning its reputation once more where the historicist faith is concerned. More specifically, I think the argument from complexity suggests the following: the greater the number of structures something may have, then, other things being equal, the lesser are the chances of any one structure's persisting indefinitely, especially as the predominant or principal structure; and the greater the number of structures something may have, the more remote are the chances that all of these structures will be morally desirable—at least some part or aspect of any whole, process, or trend is apt to be undesirable or to have undesirable consequences.

Individual persons may belong to, or be part of, one or more wholes, processes, or trends that are incompatible with one another (have conflicting structures); and when this incompatibility is forced home upon the individual, when, for example, he has a moral crisis in choosing between them, it is especially difficult to anticipate which way he will go. It is well known that Marxists expected individual members of the lower middle classes to embrace socialism during the economic and social dislocations that followed World War I, but a significant number of them chose fascism instead; on my analysis, this might be explained either in terms of their belonging to more than one social or cultural whole or in terms of the social or cultural whole to which they did belong being structured in more than just one way. The lower middle classes in Germany, for example, undoubtedly included the following: (1) patriots and war veterans who were embittered by Germany's defeat, some of whom were looking for scapegoats to blame for this defeat and who found such scapegoats in radicals, socialists, and Jews; (2) individuals who were especially hard hit by the economic and social dislocations of the postwar period, and we know (from social science and history) that such persons are frequently attracted to charismatic, savior personalities who promise to confer a sense of order and of personal worth upon individuals who at a previous time actually possessed some such sense of well-being; and (3) individuals who had lost their religion or were in the process of losing it, but who still missed the authority and consolations of the Church and wished to obey *someone*. Individuals belonging to one or more of these groups might be more willing to follow someone like Hitler than to obey the dictates of something called "economic self-interest." Here one could say either that a significant or influential number of members of the lower middle class also belonged to other social groups or wholes and that this membership was decisive in falsifying Marxist expectations that the lower middle class would gradually be absorbed by and identify with the proletariat; or one could say that the lower middle class taken as a structured whole or as a part of a structured whole (Germany) possessed a number of different structures, or participated in a number of different structures, some of which inclined their members to move to the right politically rather than to the left.

Several general "lessons" can be drawn from the above example. First, it suggests ways in which the behavior of individuals (always the "rock bottom" element in any social or historical explanation, at least according to methodological individualists such as Popper) might be explained by some obviously nontrivial laws, including laws about structured wholes, processes, and trends. Second, it reminds us of what Popper had to say about the "logic of the situation," but where the *explanation* of the behavior in question is concerned the operative variable seems to be not some "objective" logic of the situation so much as the values and beliefs an individual agent brings with him to the assessment of his situation. Third, while these two "lessons" may go more against Popper than in his favor, the argument from the complexity of the world which I have attributed to Popper on the basis of his remarks about wholes, properties, and structures seems amply borne out by the above example. Complexity does not make for those "differences in kind" so dear to the hearts of either/or philosophers, but it does serve to remind us of how hazardous and difficult the prediction of human behavior actually is, especially when we are dealing with the question of under what conditions certain trends in human behavior will persist.

CHAPTER FOUR

The Dualism of Facts and Standards

But does history have *meaning?*

Here we may recall briefly W. H. Walsh's distinction between "meaning in history" and "meaning of history" and his further distinction between two kinds of "meaning of history." Popper obviously believes that there is meaning in history, that particular historical phenomena are intelligible, although this belief may be qualified by his insistence upon both the "triviality" of the covering laws and the "circularity" of the interpretations historians use to explain particular historical phenomena. While particular historical phenomena can be explained, there cannot be, according to Popper, any laws (presumably not even any trivial laws) that cover history taken as a whole or as a "unique" process, and thus he believes there can be no "meaning of history" of the first kind noted by Walsh. Moreover, even if there *could* be a "meaning of history" in the sense of there being laws of history (as I have argued *contra* Popper that there could be), there could not be any "meaning of history" for Popper where Walsh's second kind of "meaning of history" is concerned (except as something we bring to history); in other words, moral meaning cannot be read off or inferred from historical reality or from empirical or factual statements we may make about historical reality. I think Popper is basically correct here, whether we are concerned with the moral meaning of particular historical phenomena or with the moral meaning of history taken as a whole or as a unique process. Popper's insistence upon the "dualism of facts and decisions," or "facts and policies" or "facts and standards," is an expression of a belief in the autonomy of our moral decision making, and as such it seems to me a highly significant challenge to historicism conceived of as a moral philosophy.

Popper regards historicism as an abdication of moral responsibility and as a species of moral futurism. The connection between these allegations is, I think, roughly that historicism passes the moral buck to the future. Marxism, Hegelianism, and even some versions of Christianity are corrupted, according to Popper, by the belief that the reason or at least one reason why their cause is just is that it is certain to prevail; and this belief has the undesirable result of releasing the individual from moral responsibility for his decisions and actions. The future is on our side, history will justify our conduct, and besides nothing we can do will alter the course or direction of history: all these judgments or slogans seem to Popper to be expressions of the old, highly immoral thesis that might makes right.

In order to isolate what it is in historicism as a moral philosophy that Popper takes exception to, it might at this point be helpful to make some distinction between morality and prudence. Although Popper to my knowledge does not employ the word 'prudence,' his moral philosophy owes much to Kant who did, of course, attempt to distinguish between prudence and morality. Popper speaks approvingly of Kant's "Copernician Revolution" in the field of ethics which he locates in "Kant's doctrine of autonomy—the doctrine that we cannot accept the command of an authority, however exalted, as the ultimate basis of ethics";[1] and if Popper does not explicitly employ Kant's distinction between prudence and morality he does explicitly endorse Kant's views concerning the equality of men, Kant's distinction between moral autonomy and heteronomy, and Kant's categorical imperative, which he presents as " 'always recognize that human individuals are ends and do not use them as mere means to your ends.' "[2] (I shall have more to say about these topics later.) In defending his thesis that in scientific methodology we should attempt to find out what scientists *ought* to do, as contrasted with deciding what they in fact do, Popper writes: "This 'ought' is not a matter of ethics (though ethics comes in, too) but rather the 'ought' of a hypothetical imperative."[3] Popper recommends to the scientist that he ought to proceed by the method of conjecture and refutation, and in characterizing this 'ought' as the 'ought' of a hypothetical imperative Popper apparently has in mind Kant's distinction between a hypothetical and a categorical imperative. Popper is not recommending that everybody, or everybody in certain kinds of situations, should study science, nor is he even saying that every scientist ought to use the method of conjecture and refutation—at least he is not saying this in the same categorical or unconditional way in which he would say that we ought always to recognize that human individuals are ends and not

1. *Conjectures and Refutations,* 181.
2. *The Open Society and Its Enemies,* I, 102, 256; II, 385.
3. "Replies to My Critics," 1031.

mere means to our ends. Rather he is saying something like, "If you wish to contribute most effectively to the advancement of science, you ought to use the method of conjecture and refutation." And one place where Popper presumably would think that "ethics comes in, too" would be in one's choice or decision to commit oneself to the advancement of science.

While a detailed comparison of the ethics of Popper and Kant lies outside the scope of the present inquiry, the following conclusions seem warranted. (1) The way in which Popper employs Kant's distinction between hypothetical and categorical imperatives suggests the presence in Popper's philosophy of something very much like Kant's distinction between morality and prudence, even if Popper does not use the word 'prudence' and even if the refinements present in Kant's treatment of the relationships between prudence and morality are lacking. (2) Popper, like Kant, does not despise prudence or a reasonable concern for one's future well-being and happiness; rather he encourages prudence where it assists us in making intelligent, informed moral choices and when it involves calculating how best to do what one has chosen to do. (3) However, for Popper, as for Kant, morality still ranks above prudence because only morality can inform us as to whether our choices are fully (categorically) justifiable. Although, as we shall see, there are some significant differences between Popper and Kant where deciding what is morally justifiable is concerned, I think they would be in complete agreement that there may be cases, "unjust war" situations, for example, where it is not morally right to choose to become a scientist or where, if that choice has already been made, it is not morally right to use what one believes to be the optimal scientific method, whether it be the one recommended by

Popper or some other. Not doing science or not doing it well could become one's moral duty, even if one's future success or one's very life was at stake.

From what Popper actually does say about social policy and social engineering, I think he would want to distinguish between genuine and spurious prudence. To judge from some of his examples in *The Poverty of Historicism,* he would probably say that prudence has its rightful place when we are contemplating building a shelter capable of withstanding a typhoon or when we are considering a new business venture—here we have, respectively, technology and market analyses to rely upon—but prudence is simply not possible where the course or direction of history is concerned—here there is nothing comparable to the information that technology or market analysis can supply. The reasons prudence would be spurious where the course or direction of history is concerned are to be found mainly in Popper's treatment of trends and wholes, which I discussed in the previous chapter. History is not something we can be prudent about, as we can be prudent about typhoons and risky business ventures because, according to Popper, history (taken as a whole) does not exist. I think, however, that even if Popper were somehow persuaded that history taken as a whole (either as a totality or as a structured whole) does exist and that the successful prediction of trends for history taken as a whole, in one of these two senses, is feasible, he would still deny that this bridges the gap between prudence and morality and between 'is' and 'ought.' The second thing he might want to say about prudence is this: not only does historicism encourage a spurious kind of prudence, advising us to get on the winning side of history when in fact we can never be certain what the winning side will be, but historicism actually discourages us from the legitimate use of prudence, as, for example, in piecemeal social engineering, by teaching us that nothing we can do will alter our historical fate or destiny. In *The Poverty of Historicism* Popper maintains that historicism has encouraged both activism and a peculiar variety of fatalism, activism as a way of acquiescing in and helping certain "impending changes" to occur and "fatalism in regard to the trends of history."[4] I have discussed this claim earlier; here I think Popper's essential position can be expressed as follows: whether historicism encourages or discourages action on our part, it does so in large measure by claiming to possess a knowledge of the future that it does not and, according to Popper, cannot possess. Moreover, the specific activities the historicist recommends will be of exactly the wrong sort, encouraging us to assist certain very general, overall trends in coming about or persisting (just the sort of thing where individual effort is likely to count for nothing and where concerted social effort may result in unintended consequences of great magnitude and possibly great harm), while discouraging us from more modest individual and social efforts (where the analogy with controlled scientific experiment can have some real force, where the chances of success may be greater than in the case of wholesale "experiments," and where at least it is far easier to learn from—and correct—our mistakes).

Conceived of as a moral philosophy, historicism suffers, I think Popper would say, from three basic deficiencies. First, it is immoral because it teaches us to substitute an indecent concern with what the future will be like for the resolve to do what is

4. *The Poverty of Historicism*, 48–52.

morally right. Second, for all its concern with being on the winning side of history, it is actually imprudent because it teaches us to refrain from attempting just those (piecemeal) social and economic changes we have the best chances of making successfully. Third, it is illogical because it ignores the "dualism of facts and decisions" or of "facts and standards." I wish now to consider the third point, but, since Popper says very little about this dualism in the concluding pages of *The Open Society and Its Enemies* or even in the Addenda, "Facts, Standards, and Truth: A Further Criticism of Relativism," which he added in 1961, its importance for his answer to the question of whether history has any meaning could easily be overlooked or misunderstood. Accordingly, I shall begin by trying to locate or place this dualism in a more general philosophical perspective or point of view which, I believe, Popper shares with Kant.

The essentially Kantian cast of Popper's moral philosophy is implicit in his claim that "historicism, with its substitution of certainty for hope, must lead to a moral futurism."[5] Since Popper believes that philosophers have traditionally (and wrongly) tended to equate certainty with knowledge, I think this passage could be read simply as a reaffirmation of Popper's fallibilism both in epistemology and ethics; however, I believe that we can also find in the above quotation echoes of Kant's three great questions, What can I know?, What ought I to do?, and, What may I hope for? While Popper is severely critical of Kant for claiming too much for epistemology (he alleges that according to Kant's theory of knowledge our discovery of the laws of nature is necessary, but denies that this

5. *The Open Society and Its Enemies,* II, 274.

can be the case—the truth, according to Popper, is never "manifest"),[6] Popper and Kant are agreed that questions about knowledge are to be sharply distinguished from questions concerning what one should do and what one may hope for. For Kant, the question 'What ought I to do?' is entirely practical, while the question 'What may I hope for?' is at once practical and theoretical. Here 'practical' is to be taken in Kant's broad sense to include both practical and moral matters, or as he wrote, "everything that is possible through freedom."[7] Kant's use of 'theoretical' in this connection is more complicated: we "know" God and His laws not in the sense in which we know the objects of scientific inquiry and their laws, but rather as a Being whose existence is a necessary condition of the moral life; hoping is concerned with happiness, and happiness is an end or goal of morality (though since every man already has his own happiness as his end it would be odd to say that he has a *duty* to seek what he inevitably and spontaneously pursues); and ultimately we must, according to Kant, trust God to see to it that the morally good man will receive, here or in the afterlife, the happiness he deserves.[8] Since I am using Kant only to clarify certain aspects of Popper's thought, I shall not discuss the special problems posed by Kant's "moral faith" or by his doctrine of freedom, in which he attempts, unsuccessfully in Popper's judgment, to distinguish between the noumenal self, which he believed is free, and the phenomenal self, which like all

6. *Conjectures and Refutations,* 95; *The Poverty of Historicism,* 157.

7. *The Critique of Pure Reason,* A800, B828 (translated by Norman Kemp Smith).

8. For an eloquent denial of the thesis that this makes God into a divine paymaster, see Allen W. Wood, *Kant's Moral Religion* (Ithaca, N.Y., 1970).

phenomena seems bound to obey the laws of nature. Also, I shall not discuss Popper's views on religion, although the variety of historicism under discussion when Popper made the remark quoted above about certainty, hope, and moral futurism happened to be a Christian historicism (that the meek will inherit the earth was being offered, according to Popper, as evidence of the moral rectitude of the meek). Despite his great respect for the Christian ethic (in its pure, nonhistoricist form), Popper is a secular humanist, and for him both 'What ought I to do?' and 'What may I hope for?' would be practical questions in Kant's sense of 'practical.' (Popper uses 'practical' in this way when he speaks of "Kant's central practical doctrine" that individuals are ends and not mere means.)[9] While a very abstract parallel can be noted between Kant's moral religion and Popper's efforts to distinguish the moral content of Christianity from what he takes to be its obscurantist and authoritarian aspects, and while there is clearly a resemblance between the *intention* of Kant's doctrine of freedom and that of Popper's "indeterminism," the essential resemblance to note here is that both Kant and Popper believe there are real alternatives or choices open to us when we confront the questions of what we ought to do and what we may hope for in a way in which such alternatives or choices are not open to us where questions of science and empirical fact are concerned. Kant's way of putting this is that "although reason does indeed have causality in respect of freedom in general, it does not have causality in respect of nature as a whole; and although moral principles of reason can indeed give rise to free actions, they cannot give rise to laws of nature."[10] For Popper, while it is true that we *decide*

9. *The Open Society and Its Enemies,* I, 102.
10. *Critique of Pure Reason,* A808, B836.

to adopt, tentatively, a hypothesis or proposition that states a fact, or law of nature, there is this important difference: "the proposal to adopt a policy or standard, its discussion, and the decision to adopt it, may be said to *create* this policy or this standard. On the other hand, the proposal of a hypothesis, its discussion, and the decision to adopt it—or to accept a proposition—does not, in the same sense, create a fact."[11] We are not free to accept or reject the laws of nature in the sense in which we are free, according to both Kant and Popper, to select the principles or standards of our conduct and to act upon such principles or standards.

The above discussion suggests one further possibility that I shall mention although it runs counter to Popper's disdain for language analysis and his suspicion of arguments couched in terms of "category mistakes." Popper's claim that historicism substitutes (spurious) certainty for (reasonable) hope concerning our future can be read as involving something more than the allegation that historicism is simply too ambitious—knowledge or certainty (Popper could have said) is being claimed of future states of human affairs when the appropriate categories for such future states are hope, decision, and effort. The concluding paragraph of *The Open Society and Its Enemies* begins, "Instead of posing as prophets we must become the makers of our fate."[12] There is, obviously, moral

11. *The Open Society and Its Enemies,* II, 383.

12. Ibid., 280. For Popper's objections to Gilbert Ryle's notion of a category mistake, see *Conjectures and Refutations,* 302–303. Where the mind-body relation is concerned Popper seems to be saying, *contra* Ryle, that ordinary English is dualistic (at least this is how I interpret his remark that "ordinary English very often treats mental states and physical states on a par with each other" [ibid., 302]), but even if it were not dualistic I think Popper would say this would be inconclusive as an argument against mind-body dualism. I am not entirely certain of this, however. In "Language and the Body-Mind Problem" (1953)

exhortation here, but this in part reflects Popper's belief that hope, decision, and effort can make a difference where our future is concerned in a way in which they can not make a difference where the laws of nature are concerned. To be sure, Popper believes that modest, small-scale predictions of the results of human hopes, decisions, and efforts have been successfully made, in economics and technology, for example; and it is obvious that future states of some physical phenomena are affected by our decisions, although such alterations could scarcely be regarded as changes in the laws of nature.

I shall not discuss in any detail some interesting developments in Popper's later philosophy in which he argues that there are "three worlds," the physical world, the mental world, and the world of ideas, except to note that if these worlds interact, as he believes they do, then, according to Popper, some degree of "indeterminism" is a necessary condition for such interaction to occur. "Determinism" would, Popper maintains, require "the causal closure of world 1 against world 2," whereas Popper (who is a kind of dualist but not an epiphenomalist where the mind-body relation is concerned) thinks it obvious that (a) our mental activities do somehow make a difference in the physical world and (b) the world of

---

Popper wrote that because there are two languages, a physical and a psychological one, which are not mutually translatable, it follows that they "deal with different kinds of facts" or phenomena (ibid., 294); but in "A Note on the Body-Mind Problem" (1955) he seems to realize that this move from language to ontology was too quick, especially for someone who is skeptical about language analysis. He writes, "Assuming that, by the usage of our language, expressions naming physical states are put in a category different from that in which expressions naming mental states are put, I should be inclined to see in this fact an indication, or a suggestion (not more than this, to be sure), that these two categories of expression name entities which are *ontologically* different—or in other words, that they are *different kinds of entities*" (ibid., 302).

ideas—scientific theories, for example—exerts an immense though indirect influence upon the physical world (world 1) through the mental world (world 2), as in the case of technology. The mental world or "mental states" mediate between world 3 (the world of ideas) and world 1. (World 3, while "objective," is "man made" and does not act directly upon world 1—Popper believes that this distinguishes his "world 3" from the third-world doctrines he associates with Plato and Hegel.)[13] All of this seems highly abstract and speculative, as Popper himself realizes; and it is obvious, as I think he might acknowledge, that the same argument that requires "indeterminism" to prevent a complete causal closure of world 1 against world 2 also requires some minimal sort of determinism if world 3, through the intervention or mediation of world 2, is to have "an immense influence" upon world 1. Here 'intervention,' 'mediation,' and 'influence' are clearly causal concepts; and, if we are to take seriously Popper's three-worlds hypothesis, mental activity must be seen as somehow causally efficacious in bringing about changes in the physical world. Even more obviously, cause-effect relations must continue to obtain *within* the physical world unless the effect of mental activity upon physical phenomena is to be curiously limited. I don't think Popper would object to this minimal or weaker version of determinism (although he might object to my choice of words) because, so far as I can tell, his strictures against "determinism" are not directed either against interactionism conceived of as a theory about the causal relation between the mental and the physical, or against the thesis that 'Every event has a cause,' a thesis Popper believes to be "so

13. *Objective Knowledge,* 153–161; "Replies to My Critics," 1055–1056.

vague, that it is perfectly compatible with physical indeterminism."[14] Popper writes:

I have come more and more to the opinion that what is at stake, in the problem of indeterminism, is the problem of *the causal closure of world 1 against world 2.* Or in other words: is (the physical) world 1 (which may be deterministic or indeterministic) causally changed or causally influenced by (the mental) world 2? It is clear that if world 1 is completely deterministic, it will also be closed (and world 2, if existing at all, will be an epiphenomenal world). But even if world 1 is not deterministic—containing probabilistic propensities, for example—it still could conceivably be closed; the indeterminism of world 1 by no means implies that it is under the influence of world 2, even though indeterminism is, it seems to me, a necessary condition for there to be such an influence.[15]

This passage is helpful in locating the problem to which Popper's discussion of determinism versus indeterminism is directed, although it is rather too narrow a formulation of this problem. For example, it leaves untouched the question whether world 2 is "closed" against being causally affected by world 1—Popper apparently believes that it is not[16]—and this

14. See "Of Clouds and Clocks," *Objective Knowledge,* 220.

15. "Replies to My Critics," 1055.

16. "I am not a physicalist, even though I think that it is perfectly compatible with my position that nothing—not even problem solving—exists without a physicalist 'basis' of some sort. But 'basis' is a consciously vague term, and I regard it as possible that on the level of organisms, the relation between worlds 1 and 2, and between worlds 2 and 3 may be one of give-and-take; it may have the character of a genuine interaction" ("Replies to My Critics," 1078). In "Of Clouds and Clocks" Popper recommends that, like Descartes, we should adopt a dualistic outlook, but that instead of talking of two kinds of interacting substances we speak of "*two kinds of interacting states* (or events), physicochemical and mental ones" (*Objective Knowledge,* 252).

question is of interest to philosophers of history, as social phenomena are commonly believed to have both mental and physical aspects. Traditionally the issue of determinism has been thought to turn on whether all events (in worlds 1 *and* 2) are causally determined or whether, to use Watkins's phrase, "local pockets of randomness" exist. Popper believes such pockets do exist—both in the physical world, where he thinks probability propensities actually exist (this has the consequence that probability hypotheses in science need not always be regarded as signs of our failure to discover universal causal laws),[17] and in the mental world, where he thinks the phenomenon of creativity must be taken seriously and not just metaphorically.

Although Popper's "indeterminism" applies to worlds 1 and 2, I have suggested that one of his primary objectives in defending indeterminism is recognizably Kantian; and this reading of Popper is supported by what Popper has to say in his essay "On the Status of Science and Metaphysics." While taking care to reject Kant's determinism, he argues that "Kant was in his fundamental intention an indeterminist: even though he believed in determinism with respect to the phenomenal world as an unavoidable consequence of Newton's theory, he never doubted that man, as a moral being, was not determined. Kant never succeeded in solving the resulting conflict between his theoretical and practical philosophy in a way that satisfied him completely, and he despaired of ever finding a real solution."[18] Popper's indeterminism should be

17. For a (in my judgment, unconvincing) defense of the claim that probability propensities can be regarded as evidence for indeterminism, see J. W. N. Watkins, "The Unity of Popper's Philosophy," *The Philosophy of Karl Popper,* I, 371–412.

18. *Conjectures and Refutations,* 199.

regarded as the basis of his attempt to avoid Kant's fate not by denying the differences between theory and practice—as historicists and relativists in their various ways usually do—but by showing that the respects in which facts are determined and decisions are not determined need not result in that dichotomy between the phenomenal world, including the phenomenal self, and the moral self which Kant was unable to resolve. I shall not in this book attempt to decide whether Popper's indeterminism achieves the result he intends, although I shall give some reasons for supposing that it does not. Here let me say only that while indeterminism is the basis for Popper's attempt to succeed where Kant failed, indeterminism is in Popper's judgment only a necessary and not a sufficient condition for the existence of human freedom: as Popper makes clear in the essay "Of Clouds and Clocks," his doctrine of indeterminism needs supplementing with "a new theory of evolution" and "a new model of the organism" in which the organism in its higher functions exercises a kind of "plastic control" over its lower functions and has a "feed-back" from them. In other words, sheer chance or randomness is not enough, since the organism must have some control over what it does and, to avoid what Popper calls the nightmare of determinism, this control must be plastic and in some respects at least discretionary.[19]

The most explicit application of Popper's indeterminism to the philosophy of history occurs in the preface he added in 1957 to *The Poverty of Historicism,* but since I regard the

19. *Objective Knowledge,* 206–255. For some doubts concerning Popper's claim that he can solve the mind-body problem "without saying *what* 'mind' or 'consciousness' is" (ibid., 250), see Alastair Hannay, "Freedom and Plastic Control," *Canadian Journal of Philosophy,* 2 (1972), 277–296.

argument Popper presents there as unsuccessful, I shall comment on it only briefly and mainly as a way of rounding out my interpretation of Popper as believing that the future course of human history is an object of hope, not of knowledge. The argument Popper advances in the 1957 preface is based upon his "Indeterminism in Quantum Physics and in Classical Physics,"[20] in which he argued for an indeterministic reading of both quantum and classical physics. In this paper he wrote, "We shall take indeterminism to be a doctrine asserting that *not all* events are 'determined in every detail' (whatever this may mean), and determinism as asserting that they *all* are, without exception, whether future, present, or past. . . . indeterminism does not, perhaps, assert that all or most events are not determined, but only that some events which are not completely determined exist—however rare they may be."[21] Complete foreknowledge of an event, according to Popper, implies that "the event was predetermined";[22] and since in one important case, that of scientific calculators, whether they be machines or scientists, it is logically impossible for any such calculator to have foreknowledge of all its own future results, it follows, Popper maintains, that some events are not predetermined and that Laplacean or complete determinism is mistaken. In the preface to *The Poverty of Historicism* Popper claims to have shown that "for strictly logical reasons it is impossible for us to predict the future course of history."[23] This alleged proof turns on the claim that we cannot predict the future growth of human knowledge,

20. *British Journal for the Philosophy of Science,* 1 (1950), 117–133, and 173–195.
21. Ibid., 120.
22. Ibid., 121.
23. *The Poverty of Historicism,* vi.

including scientific knowledge; since science affects the course of human history, we cannot predict the future course of human history. While it may in a sense be true, as Popper claims, that *"we cannot anticipate today what we shall know only tomorrow"*[24] where the what in question is construed in a very specific and detailed fashion, his argument leaves unaffected, I believe, the possibility of general predictions concerning the overall direction which under certain conditions science, and society insofar as it is influenced by science, will follow. In other words, indeterminism, even if it were correct, simply could not yield the result that general predictions of the future course of history are impossible. (Indeterministic interpretations of quantum physics, while denying the possibility of predicting the behavior of subatomic particles on the micro level, usually acknowledge that predictions on the macro or aggregate level are still possible, and Popper in his article on indeterminism does not reject this possibility.)

Popper maintains that his argument "does not, of course, refute the possibility of every kind of social prediction; on the contrary it is perfectly compatible with the possibility of testing social theories—for example, economic theories—by way of predicting that certain developments will take place under certain conditions. It only refutes the possibility of predicting historical developments to the extent to which they may be influenced by the growth of our knowledge."[25] But he fails to see how damaging this alleged refutation can be, and how strongly reminiscent of anti-naturalistic historicism it is: since virtually all human behavior (including, one might suppose,

24. Ibid., vii.
25. Ibid.

especially the behavior studied by the social science Popper seems to respect the most, economics) may be influenced by the growth of our knowledge, the perfect compatibility of this version of indeterminism with the testing of *any* social theories may be questioned. (In both the text of *The Poverty of Historicism* and in the "Indeterminism" article Popper discusses the "Oedipus effect," the influence of a prediction upon the predicted event, and in the "Indeterminism" article, page 189, he attempts explicitly to extend this argument about the impossibility of complete self-information from the social sciences to physics. However, the importance he attaches to the so-called Oedipus effect seems to differ significantly in the two texts. In *The Poverty of Historicism* the "Oedipus effect" argument was treated as an anti-naturalistic historicist argument aimed, unsuccessfully in Popper's judgment, against the possibility of detailed predictions in the social sciences, while in the "Indeterminism" paper he uses the Oedipus effect to show that there will be for any calculator predictive questions about itself which it will be unable to answer correctly. The "Oedipus effect" seems to have in Popper's reflections on physics exactly the result Popper had argued it should not have where the possibility of predictions in the social sciences is concerned!) Thus, even those modest, small-scale social predictions Popper defends in the text of *The Poverty of Historicism* and *The Open Society and Its Enemies* are jeopardized by what is essentially an overstated argument. Whatever the Oedipus effect does or does not show about the ultimate issue of indeterminism, we should recognize that the growth of knowledge, through published predictions of how people will behave, in elections for example, need not affect the reliability of such predictions, provided we have some knowledge of what the reaction function will be.[26] While it is always possible for people to modify their behavior in the light of predictions of what that behavior will be, and projections of reaction functions can always be reacted against, in practice social scientists have not found this to be an insuperable obstacle in the path of valid predictions. Thus, even if all or virtually all historical developments are influenced by the growth of knowledge, this in itself does not refute the possibility of their being predicted in advance.

Whatever we may think concerning the ultimate success or failure of Popper's philosophy of history, we should, I believe, applaud his intention of avoiding both an absolutistic historicism that dogmatically claims to infer the moral meaning of history from the facts of history and a historicist relativism that tends to transform questions of fact into questions of value or meaning and that urges us not to worry about choosing rationally among a plurality of historical interpretations and "meanings" of history. It is only against the background of Popper's struggles against historicism and relativism that we can appreciate the nontriviality and, I hope, essential correctness of Popper's claim that we give moral meaning to history and that we can do this legitimately because, within certain

26. See Herbert A. Simon, "Bandwagon and Underdog Effects of Election Predictions," *Public Opinion Quarterly,* 18 (1954), 245–253. There is a useful discussion of Popper's indeterminism and his philosophy of science in general in Robert John Ackermann's *The Philosophy of Karl Popper* (Amherst, Mass., 1976), and there is an extensive development of Popper's case for mind-body interactionism in *The Self and Its Brain,* written by Popper and John C. Eccles (New York, 1977). I regret that my book was written before these two works appeared and that I was unable to include a discussion of them.

physical and social limitations, we make history. The nontriviality of Popper's activist account of historical meaning can be brought out somewhat by the following example. Imagine that we say of a painting of a landscape, or of a landscape, that it is "beautiful" or "inspiring," but we do not feel sufficiently inspired to do anything, either to paint another picture or to improve upon any actual landscape. All we have is the nice, warm glow that passive appreciation affords. I suppose we could say that our judgment that the painting or the landscape is beautiful or inspiring had conferred aesthetic meaning upon it and that apart from such judgments the painting or the landscape has no aesthetic meaning or significance. But if this is all that happens here, how different it is from the case of the moral meaning of history where, according to Popper, the meaning in question stems from and contributes to our practical, moral involvement in changing the world so that some portion of it can better accommodate the goals or ends that we bring to the world.

Some historicists might complain that theirs is also an activist account of meaning, that their search for the meaning of history and their involvement in changing the world are mutually supportive activities, and that if it is activism we are looking for we should forget about Popper, for what could be more stultifying than his constant harping upon the dangers of the unintended consequences of intentional human activities? While there is some truth in this, two major qualifications need noting. (1) Although some historicists may claim to bring meaning to history, it is surely more typical of them to claim to discover it in history and to limit their activism to just those activities that will actualize or reveal a meaning already implicit or latent in the historical process. Assuming briefly for the sake of the argument that Hegel and Marx were, as Popper alleges, historicists, I think it is arguable that their respective conceptions of the historical process as the *unfolding* of freedom and their famous, or notorious, respect for the limits "historical reality" places upon responsible action fit a discovery theory of the moral meaning of history more than they do a constructionist one.[27] (2) While, obviously, Popper is in his politics more conservative than Marx and less conservative than Hegel, his concern over the unintended consequences of human behavior does not stultify all actions or even all social planning.[28] Conservative liberals *can* act, and their "creed" tells them, far less equivocally than the Marxist or Hegelian creeds, that they *should* act, for, unlike Marxists and Hegelians, they have no reason to believe that history, the historical process, will do their work or solve their problems for them, all in due if unspecified time. What separates Popper significantly from the historicist is not his concern with the unintended consequences of human conduct, since everyone who is rational recognizes that there are such consequences and

27. Jack Meiland, in *Scepticism and Historical Knowledge* (New York, 1965), contrasts discovery and constructionist theories about the nature of historical inquiry, and I believe that the contrast he develops can be extended to the debate concerning the moral meaning of history. Popper (and I) could be said to hold a discovery theory where inquiry into the facts of history is concerned, but a constructionist theory about the moral meaning of history.

28. Readers of Popper's "Autobiography" (*The Philosophy of Karl Popper,* I, 23–29), will note that Popper was, briefly as a teenager, a Marxist, and that he was alienated from Marxism by a demonstration in Vienna in which several unarmed young socialist and communist workers were killed. As a Marxist, Popper felt partly responsible for their deaths, since Marxist theory demands that the class struggle be intensified. However, since I find it doubtful whether Marxist theory demands that unarmed workers be sacrificed as a way of intensifying the class struggle, this episode in Popper's life could be interpreted as his first politically significant experience of the unintended consequences of intentional human actions.

that they are to be counted among the limitations of effective human action. The great philosophical difference between Popper and the historicist is the one noted earlier, namely, the difference between hope and certainty where our future is concerned. (Of course, there is the substantive difference between Popper and historicists over what they want the future to be like, but this is a contingent difference: it is conceivable that one could be a historicist *and* a believer in the open society, and indeed some nineteenth-century liberals who were certain that liberal democratic institutions would come to prevail universally were probably in this respect historicists.) The historicist's certainty that history must move in a given direction results in or contributes to his belief that there is a moral meaning in history, that, for example, the class struggle or the Cunning of Reason will contribute to the advance of freedom even if we in our individual capacity do not. (Hegel's standing as a historicist is jeopardized because he, unlike some Hegelians, had little to say about the future—he believed he could tell us what the Cunning of Reason had done, not what it will do.) However, since the historicist is usually certain where history is going and that it will actualize just those goals or ends that are in his judgment morally desirable, he believes we should, if we wish to be effective, act in harmony with the dictates of history, secure in the conviction that posterity will approve of what we have done. By contrast the Popperian ethic affirms that "we must be taught to do our work, to make our sacrifice for the sake of this work, and not for praise or the avoidance of blame. . . . We must find our justification in our work, in what we are doing ourselves, and not in a fictitious 'meaning of history'."[29]

29. *The Open Society and Its Enemies,* II, 278.

I do not propose to compare in detail Popper's reflections on the philosophy of history with those contained in Kant's "Idea of a Universal History from a Cosmopolitan Point of View,"[30] but the basic resemblance between Popper and Kant is striking. There are, of course, differences in vocabulary: Popper speaks of "meaning" and "interpretation," while Kant does not use these terms; and Kant regards an eventual federation of states as the "inevitable" result of the mutual antagonisms of men. Kant was obviously more optimistic than Popper concerning the future and more determined than Popper to place a progressive interpretation upon the results of the mutual antagonisms of men, but I doubt whether Kant's belief that a federation of states was "inevitable" is evidence that Kant was inclined toward historicism. Here we must distinguish between Kant the scientist or historian predicting what the future will be like, if the condition of mutual antagonism among states prevails, and Kant the moral philosopher; and I suggest that when Kant is speaking of the inevitability of a federation of states, it is a *moral* inevitability or necessity he has in mind rather than any pseudoscientific historicist prophecy of the sort Popper would deplore. Unless this suggestion is correct, then the tone of moral exhortation which permeates Kant's essay would seem misplaced and his remark that the idea that history will take a certain direction may "help to further its realization" would seem only a naive example of a self-fulfilling prophecy. Perhaps a more serious obstacle confronting a Popperian reading of Kant's essay is Kant's penchant for talking of "nature's purpose" for man, of what nature has "willed" that man will do, and of "the history of the human race viewed as a whole . . . as the

30. Translated by W. Hastie in *Theories of History,* ed. Patrick Gardiner (Glencoe, Ill., 1959), 22–34.

realization of a hidden plan of nature" to bring about a perfect political constitution for man. However, since for Kant, nature, like God, is not an object of possible experience, we should not read Kant as affirming that we can know something called nature and its plans and purposes, as presumably we can know individual persons and their plans and purposes. Thus Kant's talk about nature's plans and purposes should be read, but not dismissed, as anthropomorphic or metaphorical: the point of this way of talking is to make us see that a perfect political constitution is needed if man is fully to actualize his potentials for a free and rational existence.

Kant believed that we can find ends in nature and in history, that is, physical and social arrangements and structures which are conducive to the attainment and maintenance of certain end states, but he did not believe we can discover final ends in nature or in history. In the *Critique of Practical Reason* and in the *Critique of Judgment* he affirmed that we discuss final ends, as we discuss God, from the moral point of view. The discovery of ends in nature, or in history, may justify our applying the concept of end to the whole of nature or the whole of history, but we cannot decide empirically whether the whole of nature or of history actually has these ends. In Kant's terminology the judgment that nature or history conceived of as a whole has certain ends is a reflective and not a determinant judgment; as such it is regulative of our ways of looking at, and behaving in, the world, but it is not constitutive, not a part of, our knowledge of the world. If we apply this to the discussion of political constitutions, I think the following results would be generally acceptable to Kant: we may make the empirical discovery that a certain kind of political constitution is conducive to certain ends (a constitutional democracy, for example, may contribute to free and open criticism and thus to the advancement of learning and science); such a discovery would justify the *application* of the concept of end to the whole of history, but whether free and open criticism and the growth of learning and science are the end of history conceived of as a whole cannot be known empirically, since history conceived of as a whole is not an object of possible experience. The question of whether history conceived of as a whole has certain ends must accordingly be treated as a question about final ends and as such must be answered from the moral point of view.

Although Popper's discussion of the difference between moral and empirical or scientific questions is extremely sketchy in comparison with Kant's, he and Kant fully agree on the characterization of a moral question as one to which empirical or scientific answers cannot be given. And while Kant and Popper employ different technical vocabularies, Popper seems in effect to be applying Kant's distinction between reflective and determinant judgments to the philosophy of history—we make interpretations of history and we give meaning to history because we have no way of knowing whether history has meaning or not.

Thus far I have emphasized the negative side of Popper's and Kant's conception of moral judgments, including judgments about the meaning of history, namely that these are judgments which empirical investigation and science cannot make for us. But for Popper, and for Kant, too, I believe, such a conception of moral judgments is mainly a positive, liberating doctrine. Popper writes:

It is the problem of nature and convention which we meet here again. Neither nature nor history can tell us what we ought to do. Facts, whether those of nature or those of history, cannot make the decision for us, they cannot determine the ends we are going to choose. It is we who introduce purpose and meaning into nature and history. Men are not equal; but we can decide to fight for equal rights. Human institutions such as the state are not rational, but we can decide to make them more rational.[31]

Here Popper quickly transforms a thesis about what the facts of nature and history cannot do for us into a thesis about what we can, and should, do for ourselves. "This dualism of facts and decisions," Popper continues, "is, I believe, fundamental. Facts as such have no meaning; they gain it only through our decisions."[32] In defending this dualism in the Addenda, he argues that no system of standards, including a religious system, can overcome this dualism by an appeal to authority, not even to the authority of God; and he maintains that "this is Kant's idea of autonomy, as opposed to heteronomy."[33] This sentence contains the essence of Popper's case against historicism: *historicism is heteronomous where the facts of history are concerned and attempts, unsuccessfully, to bridge the gap between facts and decisions with statements about history, and especially the "direction" of history, which, even if they could be known to be true, cannot determine the ends we are going to choose.* Of course, as a matter of psychological fact some people are persuaded that because history seems to be moving in a certain direction they should also move in that direction, so when Popper maintains that "facts" about history and its course cannot determine the ends we are going to choose he means that they cannot logically determine our choice of ends, cannot in other words provide a rationally

31. *The Open Society and Its Enemies,* II, 278.
32. Ibid., 278–279.
33. Ibid., 385.

sufficient basis for our choice of ends, which is a matter of moral decision. Later I shall discuss his arguments on behalf of a dualism between facts and decisions, but here I should note that this is not "merely" a logical issue, or at any rate not a simple or single logical issue, but rather one that is closely related to Popper's and Kant's conception of the person as a free and rational being. John Rawls gives an eloquent account of the autonomous individual as Kant pictured him: "The principles he acts upon are not adopted because of his social position or natural endowments, or in view of the particular kind of society in which he lives or the specific things he happens to want. To act on such principles is to act heteronomously."[34] If we apply this notion of acting heteronomously to the historicist, we can see him as choosing his principles and basing his decisions not upon what he believes to be right or just but in view of the particular kind of society in which he *expects* eventually to be living. And such an individual is not a person in the full, normative sense endorsed by Kant and by Popper.

In citing Rawls's interpretation of Kant, I do not intend to use the Kantian element present in both Popper's and Rawls's ethics to make Popper over into a Rawlsian. There is, for example, no discussion in Popper of a lexical or hierarchical ordering of principles of justice or of any moral principles (although Rawls's preference for liberty over equality would appeal to the classical liberal in Popper); and there is in Popper no discussion of various strategies for achieving a just society (although Rawls's maximin strategy would, I think, appeal to the conservative in Popper). Rather I wish to cite

34. *A Theory of Justice* (New York, 1971), 252.

Rawls's interpretation of Kant as a way of overcoming the one major obstacle confronting my claim that Popper is basically a Kantian in his ethics. The problem is that while Popper explicitly embraces Kant's categorical imperative, Kant gave three—or five—formulations of the categorical imperative, and Popper nowhere endorses or quotes those formulations in which Kant speaks of universalizing the maxim of one's actions or of the individual as a law-giving member in a universal kingdom of ends.[35] In other words, Popper neglects the formal, universalizing aspects of Kant's ethics, and this, I think, is deliberate. Popper writes, "(Kant was right when he based the Golden Rule on the idea of reason. To be sure, it is impossible to prove the rightness of any ethical principle, or even to argue in its favour in just the manner in which we argue in favour of a scientific statement. Ethics is not a science. But although there is no 'rational scientific basis' of ethics, there is an ethical basis of science, and of rationalism.)"[36]

Although Kant would readily have agreed that we cannot argue for an ethical principle in the way in which we argue for a scientific statement, Popper's parenthesis is disturbing to anyone who accepts the usual picture of Kant as having tried to provide a formal decision procedure for determining the rightness of an ethical principle or maxim of action.[37] The overall flavor of this parenthesis is disturbing for another reason: Popper seems here to be close to conflating 'rational' and 'scientific' when what he wants, or should want, like

35. *The Open Society and Its Enemies,* I, 102. For Kant's different formulations of the categorical imperative, see H. J. Paton, *The Categorical Imperative* (New York, 1967), 129–132.

36. *The Open Society and Its Enemies,* II, 238.

37. For a discussion of Kant's treatment of maxims of action as principles, see Paton, 58–62.

Kant, is to show how ethics can be rational without being scientific. In the Addenda, Popper in his last reference to Kant tells us that while we should seek for absolutely right or valid proposals in the realm of standards, we should never persuade ourselves that we have actually found them," for clearly, there cannot be a criterion of *absolute rightness*—even less than a criterion of absolute truth."[38] The caution concerning the possibility of error seems unexceptional and consistent with Popper's overall fallibilism, but the claim that there cannot be a criterion of absolute rightness would seem to require some revision either in the standard interpretation of Kant or in my interpretation of Popper as a Kantian.

Many complex issues in Kant, and Popper, exegesis are involved here, but I am encouraged by Rawls's suggestion that the significance of what he calls "generality and universality" in Kant's ethics has received undue emphasis and that perhaps the most important aspect of Kant's moral philosophy is his doctrine of autonomy. If this is so, then Popper's standing as a Kantian in his ethics seems once more secure, especially when his endorsement of Kant's position concerning the value of impartiality and the moral equality of individuals is also taken into account. The problem that remains is this: in the absence of a procedure, formal or otherwise, for deciding on the rightness of an ethical principle or a proposed course of action, what is to prevent autonomous behavior from becoming arbitrary behavior, and indeed can we any longer distinguish between the two? This is, I think, essentially the same problem Popper considers in connection with the

38. *The Open Society and Its Enemies,* II, 386. Popper does not mention Kant's name here, but this page is in the index under "golden rule, Kant's . . . justification of . . . ."

"dualism of nature and convention," or of "fact and decision," namely, whether 'convention' should be construed as implying 'arbitrariness.'

The Addenda to *The Open Society and Its Enemies* is, I believe, the clearest introduction we have to Popper's philosophy, especially as his epistemology and his philosophy of science bear upon his moral and political philosophy. "Facts, Standards, and Truth: A Further Criticism of Relativism" reflects Popper's intention of providing a viable alternative to the extremes of relativism and absolutism in both epistemology and moral philosophy. With this program in mind I shall try to outline briefly the main steps in Popper's argument. (1) Popper maintains that the question 'What is truth?' can be answered as follows: "an assertion, proposition, statement, or belief is true if, and only if, it corresponds to the facts."[39] He endorses Alfred Tarski's formulation of the correspondence theory of truth, which he considers to be in a sense "trivial" but informative as a reply to the skeptic or relativist who doubts that we can know what truth is. (2) For Popper, however, "knowing what truth means, or under what conditions a statement is called true, is not the same as, and must be distinguished from, possessing a means of deciding—a *criterion* for deciding—whether a given statement is true or false."[40] This is the basis for Popper's rejection of what he calls "criterion philosophies," which he considers to be a species of philosophical absolutism. It is the failure of philosophical absolutism that leads to "disappointment" and hence to relativism or skepticism. (3) What Popper calls "the kernel of

39. Ibid., 369.
40. Ibid., 371.

truth" in relativism and skepticism is that "there exists no general criterion of truth. But this does not warrant the conclusion that the choice between competing theories is arbitrary."[41] Popper's fallibilism emphasizes the possibility of error in all quests for knowledge, and also, one might say, the actuality of error in all claims to certainty. But the discovery of error provides, according to Popper, no support for relativism or skepticism, as "every discovery of a mistake constitutes a real advance in our knowledge."[42] For Popper the important thing about an error is not that a mistake has been made but that *"we can learn from our mistakes."* Popper calls this "a fundamental insight" and "the basis of all epistemology and methodology."[43] (4) Popper writes, "In all this, the idea of the growth of knowledge—of getting nearer to the truth—is decisive."[44] He gives this example: Kepler's theory contained much true information, but it was false because deviations from Kepler's ellipses do occur. Newton's theory in turn contained far more true information than Kepler's and was thus a closer approximation to the truth, although it was still a false theory. Popper's fallibilism, I believe, seeks to turn relativism or skepticism on its head: the discovery of error, instead of being the despair of those who seek knowledge, can be (a) a methodological incentive or heuristic that encourages us to search for our mistakes and to criticize our theories, and (b) the basis of a fallible, realistic epistemology, which tells us that at least "we know where the truth is not to be found." While rejecting absolutist and dogmatic claims to possess the

41. Ibid., 374.
42. Ibid., 376.
43. Ibid.
44. Ibid.

truth or at least a criterion of truth, Popper's fallibilism takes from the absolutist the idea that mistakes are "absolute mistakes in the sense that if a theory deviates from the truth, it is simply false, even if the mistake was less glaring than in another theory. Thus the notions of truth, and of falling short of the truth, can represent absolute standards for the fallibilist."[45]

I should like to interrupt my exposition at this point to express briefly two separate but related reservations about what Popper has attempted thus far. My first reservation is that, although agreeing with much of what Popper says in criticism of so-called criterion philosophies (he has in mind mainly positivism), I am concerned over the exact difference between a criterion and a standard, especially an absolute standard, and whether this difference, once we have located it, does not have more disturbing implications than Popper might wish it to have. Of course, there will be a difference in the attitude absolutists take toward criteria and the attitude fallibilists take toward standards, but this attitude, to be philosophically significant, must reflect some objective difference between criteria and standards. Tarski has shown, according to Popper, that "*there can be no general criterion of truth* (except with respect to certain artificial language systems of a somewhat impoverished kind)."[46] However, Tarski's correspondence theory of truth has often been misinterpreted as seeking to provide a criterion of truth or "*a method of deciding* whether or not a given statement is true."[47] This shows, I think, the crucial difference between a criterion and a standard

45. Ibid., 377.
46. Ibid., 375.
47. *Objective Knowledge,* 317.

of truth: a criterion of truth provides a method for deciding the truth of a statement while a standard of truth does not. (I have previously quoted Popper as denying the possibility of a general criterion either of truth or of absolute rightness: this must mean that we also lack a method of deciding on the rightness or goodness of the moral decisions, standards, or proposals Popper speaks of in defending his dualism of facts and standards.) If a standard of truth cannot do what a criterion of truth was (falsely) said to be capable of doing, it is nevertheless extremely valuable as what Popper calls "a *regulative principle* (as Kant or Peirce might have said)."[48] As "a regulative idea" the concept of truth has the following value: "It helps us in our search for truth that we know there is something like truth or correspondence. It does not give us a means of finding truth, or of being sure that we have found it even if we have found it. So there is no criterion of truth, and we must not ask for a criterion of truth. We must be content with the fact that the idea of truth as correspondence to the facts has been rehabilitated."[49] But one wonders what the rehabilitation of the idea of truth accomplishes if we cannot have a method of deciding when we have found the truth. This brings me to my second reservation, which concerns the connection Popper seeks to establish in the Addenda and elsewhere between "falling short of the truth" and "getting nearer to the truth."

The discovery that one is falling short of the truth will not, I think, necessarily bring us nearer to the truth. Assuming that the notion of "nearer to the truth" can be explicated in terms of Popper's verisimilitude (which he characterizes as a "meta-

48. *Conjectures and Refutations,* 226.
49. *Objective Knowledge,* 319.

logical idea" that will not lead to any changes in "the theory of method"), the problem of how the discovery of error gets us nearer the truth remains, I think, largely unresolved.[50] "Falling short of the truth" might well result in an endless succession of trials and errors unless we have independent reason to suppose that the number of theories to be tested is finite and that at least one of them is true.[51] I imagine Popper would probably object that this is not a criticism, but that instead I have simply called attention to a risk we do in fact run, and one which no epistemology or methodology should overlook. As he has remarked in connection with Kant's epistemology, we must beware of an epistemology that proves too much, and no epistemology or methodology can guarantee that we will discover the truth or even get nearer to the truth. This, I think, is correct as far as it goes, but it does not resolve all doubt concerning the viability of Popper's union of a fallibilist

50. See *Conjectures and Refutations,* 234. For a discussion of difficulties concerning Popper's definition of verisimilitude, see Pavil Tichý, "On Popper's Definition of Verisimilitude," and David Miller, "Popper's Qualitative Theory of Verisimilitude," *British Journal for the Philosophy of Science,* 25 (1974), 155–160 and 166–177. In "Two Kinds of Verisimilitude," a paper read at the American Philosophical Association's meeting in Boston, 1976, Clifton B. Perry distinguishes between what he calls "relative" and "absolute" verisimilitude. He argues that increase in the empirical content of scientific theories, while important for the question whether science progresses, is irrelevant for the comparison of the truth and falsity content of competing theories. In his terminology, "relative" verisimilitude can be established for commensurate theories without recourse to any nondemonstrative or ampliative principle of reasoning, and the problems that arise from the quest for "absolute" verisimilitude can be avoided. This paper seems to offer a viable way of reconciling Popper's claim that we may rationally prefer one theory over another with his further claim that in some ultimate sense, which Perry seeks to capture by speaking of "absolute" verisimilitude, all scientific theories remain guesses.

51. See Grover Maxwell, "Corroboration without Demarcation," *The Philosophy of Karl Popper,* I, 301–302.

epistemology and a falisificationist methodology. "Getting nearer to the truth" remains problematic in terms of Popper's system, in large part because of the doubts he has expressed about our ability to know when we have found the truth, if we ever do, and because of the status of his falsificationism as a method aimed essentially at telling us when we have failed to find the truth; and this problem cannot, I think, be glossed over by optimistic, progressive readings of the history of science when the very basis of such optimism is what is at issue.

The cornerstone of Popper's philosophy is the claim that "everything is open to criticism," and that while all the so-called sources of knowledge such as tradition, reason, imagination, and observation, may be used, *"none has any authority."*[52] As a consequence, a critical method for the evaluation of theories is held by Popper to be essential. Since "theories are not, in general, capable of being established or justified," *decisions* must enter the critical method, and by this Popper means that we have to make up our minds as to whether critical arguments justify the tentative acceptance of a theory or a tentative preference for one theory over its competitors.[53] The absolutist, as Popper describes him, would presumably want to deny or minimize the importance of decisions, and even if he employed a critical method he would expect critical argument to be sufficient to establish or justify some theory or other. By contrast those philosophers whom Popper calls "irrationalists and existentialists" look upon critical argument as being in all or most cases insufficient and stress the importance of decision, which they tend to look upon as "a leap in the dark" or a blind choice. This irrationalist or existentialist

52. *The Open Society and Its Enemies,* II, 378.
53. Ibid., 380.

characterization of decision seems to Popper to be an "exaggeration" or "overdramatization," based upon a disappointment over our inability to "know" without making assumptions and our inability to make assumptions without taking up what Popper here calls "a fundamental position" (and what he has in mind, I believe, when in the text of *The Open Society and Its Enemies* he speaks of "points of view").[54] Such fundamental positions, according to irrationalists and existentialists, cannot be chosen on the basis of knowledge; here Popper would presumably agree but without attaching the significance to this discovery that irrationalists and existentialists do. The critical method as described by Popper seeks to avoid the extremes of absolutism on the one hand and of irrationalism and existentialism on the other, by cautioning us not to expect too much from any "source" or any "method" (including the critical method itself), but not to turn our backs upon rational argument and open discussion even though they must fail to provide a final or absolute justification for any theory, let alone any "fundamental position" or decision.

It is Popper's discussion of decisions in general that leads into his most extended but still extremely brief treatment of the dualism of facts and standards, which he has variously described as a dualism of propositions and proposals, of facts and policies, and, initially, as a dualism of facts and decisions or norms. I think it important that he began by linking up "decisions" and "norms" in this way, and I shall note what I take to be his reason for doing so and then the reason he himself gives for abandoning this early formulation of his dualism. Decisions and norms, according to Popper, cannot be derived

54. Ibid., 380–381.

from facts, or more precisely sentences stating a decision or norm cannot be derived from a sentence stating a fact. It may be a fact that most people accept a certain norm, but this does not make this norm a fact.[55] (Popper notes that we sometimes use the term 'fact' in a "wide sense," as when we speak about "the fact that a norm is valid or right," in which case norms could be derived from facts; however, this sort of derivation does not affect the impossibility of deriving norms from what Popper calls "psychological or sociological or similar, i.e., non-semantic, facts.")[56] I think that the reason Popper in the initial formulation of his dualism contrasted decisions and norms with facts lay in his (Kantian) belief that decisions and norms are both matters of choice in a way in which facts are not. This is important, especially in the light of certain developments in moral philosophy which have occurred since he wrote *The Open Society and Its Enemies.* While philosophers for the most part are willing to grant that decisions are in some sense freely made, there is, as we shall see, a tendency in some quarters to look upon norms (or standards of conduct) as being somehow given rather than freely chosen. To be sure, decisions are, or may be, made in the light of norms, and thus norms seem to be fundamental or basic in a way in which particular decisions are not. However, the Popperian position, as I understand it, is that fundamental or basic to a point of view (or to a form of life) does not imply "not chosen" where "not chosen" means "we are not free to choose." In other words, Popper's moral man (like Kant's) is autonomous both in deciding upon courses of action and in choosing those principles or norms that will guide his decisions

55. Ibid., I, 64.
56. Ibid., 234.

and conduct; put negatively, no facts (whether they be sociological facts about what norms prevail in a given community or logical truths about the rules that are said to constitute certain activities or institutions) are in themselves sufficient to determine either our choice of norms or our decisions as to how to act in particular situations.

The reason Popper gives for abandoning the earlier formulation of his dualism in terms of 'facts' and 'decisions' or 'norms' and for preferring L. J. Russell's terminology of 'propositions' and 'proposals' is simply that "as everybody knows, one can *discuss* a proposal, while it is not so clear whether, and in what sense, one can discuss a decision or a norm; thus, by talking of 'norms' or 'decisions', one is liable to support those who say that these things are beyond discussion (either above it, as some dogmatic theologians or metaphysicians may say, or—as nonsensical—below it, as some positivists may say)."[57] I think this passage is entirely consistent with the view that Popper himself continues to believe that norms and decisions can be rationally discussed, but that he is prepared to concede an, in his judgment, empty verbal victory to those who deny that this is so—simply as a way of getting on with the discussion of how norms and decisions, which he now calls "proposals," differ from facts or propositions about facts: "we could say that a proposition may be *asserted* or *stated* (or a hypothesis *accepted*) while a proposal is adopted. . . . Our dualistic thesis then becomes the thesis that *proposals are not* reducible to *facts* (or to statements of facts, or to propositions) even though they pertain to facts."[58]

In the concluding sentence in the above quotation Popper

57. Ibid., 234.
58. Ibid., 235.

comes close to recognizing the "two senses" of 'fact' I commented on briefly in Chapter 2, and indeed this passage comes so close to distinguishing between facts as reality and facts as true statements or propositions about reality that one could not imagine Popper having any further difficulties on this score. However, in discussing the role of decision in the adoption of proposals *and* propositions, he remarks, "There is, however, an important difference here. For the proposal to adopt a policy or a standard, its discussion, and the decision to adopt it, may be said to *create* this policy or this standard. On the other hand, the proposal of a hypothesis, its discussion, and the decision to adopt it—or to accept a proposition—does not, in the same sense, create a fact."[59] The problem I see here is this: in what sense, if any, does the decision to adopt a hypothesis or accept a proposition *create* a fact? If facts are regarded as parts or aspects of reality—a view that Popper seems to reject in *Conjectures and Refutations,* but to accept in *Objective Knowledge*[60]—then it is difficult to see how prop-

59. Ibid., II, 383.

60. In *Conjectures and Refutations,* 213–214, Popper criticizes those philosophers who "believe that facts are part of the world in a sense similar to that in which processes or things may be said to be parts of the world." He maintains, rather vaguely, that "facts are something like a common product of language and reality; they are reality pinned down by descriptive statements." He goes on to claim that "new linguistic means not only help us to describe new kinds of facts; in a way, they even create new kinds of facts. In a certain sense, these facts obviously existed before the new means were created which were indispensable for their description; I say, 'obviously' because a calculation, for example, for the movement of the planet Mercury of 100 years ago, carried out today with the help of the calculus of the theory of relativity, may certainly be a true description of the facts concerned, even though the theory was not yet invented when these facts occurred. But in another sense we might say that these facts do not exist *as facts* before they are singled out from the continuum of events and pinned down by statements—the theories which describe them. These questions, however . . .

ositions about facts, or the decision to accept such propositions or statements, can in any relevant sense *create* a fact. (They *express* or *state* a fact.) For Popper's dualism the problem is acute: if proposals, policies, or standards are "created," but propositions are also in the same or some similar sense "created," then we have a resemblance that threatens to wreck, or undermine the importance of, any dualism between facts and standards. Probably this is why when Popper comes, on the very next page, to formulate "a decisive asymmetry between standards and facts," he denies, without qualification, that the decision to accept a proposition creates the cor-

---

must be left for another discussion." Popper wrote this in 1946 and did not, so far as I can tell, return to these questions, which is why they recur unresolved at a critical juncture in *The Open Society and Its Enemies,* where he is still worrying about whether facts can in some sense be said to be "created." The above passage from *Conjectures and Refutations* trades unintentionally upon the "ambiguity" of 'fact' and results in Popper's having unnecessary worries about whether certain facts existed before we had the linguistic or theoretical means to describe them: he concludes that in one sense they did but that "these facts do not exist *as facts* before they are singled out from the continuum of events and pinned down by statements," which, I think, is a misleading metaphysical or ontological way of saying that facts as reality or parts of reality exist independently of our theories but that our theories enable us to make statements of fact ('it is a fact that . . .') we could not have made before we had the theories in question. In *Objective Knowledge,* 317, in a paper written twenty years later, Popper writes, "The realist wants to have both a theory and the reality or the facts (don't call it 'reality' if you don't like it, just call it 'the facts') which are different from his theory about these facts, and which he can somehow or other then compare with the facts in order to find out whether or not it corresponds to them." This seems more acceptable, and a realist who accepts the correspondence theory of truth, as Popper and I do, must say something like this if he is to avoid that circularity of definition (truth as correspondence to the facts becoming just a way of saying that truth corresponds to true statements) which P. F. Strawson claims, wrongly in my judgment, affects the correspondence theory of truth ("Truth," in *Truth,* ed. George Pitcher [Englewood Cliffs, N.J., 1964], 42).

responding fact: "through the decision to accept a proposal (at least tentatively) we create the corresponding standard (at least tentatively); yet through the decision to accept a proposition we do *not* create the corresponding fact."[61] Of course, it was "the corresponding fact" where 'corresponding' recalls Popper's commitment to the correspondence theory of truth that concerned me when I wondered how, in any relevant sense, facts could be said to be created. I think it revealing that Popper initially seemed to want to say that there is, or could be, *some* sense in which facts may be regarded as "created," but that in the stricter formulation of his dualism he gives this up. Perhaps this is traceable ultimately to his desire to harmonize two commitments, one to the creativity of science, especially in the devising of theories that explain the behavior of various phenomena, and the other to a view which tells us that scientific theories are properly regarded as discoveries about what there is in the world and must, therefore, in some sense correspond to what there is in the world. To his credit, I think, Popper disavows pragmatism or instrumentalism as an adequate account of how scientific theories relate to "reality"—this would, obviously, be one way of honoring the first but not the second "commitment" I find in Popper.[62] Broadly speaking, I suggest that the way to harmonize these commitments is to recognize that *discovering* why things behave the way they do can be a *creative act* (and must be such if Popper's anti-inductivism turns out to be correct) without being creative in the same way in which deciding about moral norms and practical policies is "creative." And

61. *The Open Society and Its Enemies,* II, 386.
62. For Popper's criticism of instrumentalism, see "Three Views of Human Knowledge," *Conjectures and Refutations,* especially 111–114.

the way *not* to do this is to equivocate upon different senses of 'fact,' which serves neither the creativity of science nor the autonomy of ethics.

The second asymmetry Popper finds between standards and facts is that "standards always *pertain to* facts and that facts are evaluated by standards; these are relations which cannot be simply turned round."[63] Likes and dislikes, according to Popper, may play "an important role" in inducing us to accept or to reject certain standards, but nevertheless likes and dislikes belong to the realm of facts and not to the realm of standards. (In Kant's terminology, one could characterize likes and dislikes as inclinations which, although they have a part to play in the moral life, can never *determine* what our duty is.) Also, the fact that a person or a society has adopted or rejected a certain standard "must, as a fact, be distinguished from *any* standard, including the adopted or rejected standard. And since it is a fact (and an alterable fact) it may be judged or evaluated by some (other) standards."[64] Of course, it might still be objected that standards are evaluated by facts, or proposals by propositions. For example, even rather crude facts such as "I don't like it" or "We don't do things like that around here" can count as evaluations either of standards or of proposed courses of action. The Popperian reply to this would presumably be that when facts are used evaluatively they become standards or else they seem decisive only because of some tacit or implicit appeal to certain standards. Pressed hard, Popper might perhaps concede that the asymmetry between facts and standards is ultimately a *moral* asymmetry in the sense of reflecting our *decision* not to allow facts about

63. *The Open Society and Its Enemies*, II, 384.
64. Ibid.

sociology, psychology, or language usage to usurp our moral autonomy. However, he could also argue that this asymmetry is not wholly or merely ideal, but that all or most inquiries into the philosophy of language recognize some difference between prescriptive and descriptive modes of discourse; moral discourse is characteristically concerned with telling us what we should do or what attitudes we should adopt, while scientific (and historical) discourse is characteristically concerned with truthful descriptions and explanations of the behavior of various phenomena. But in this connection I think Popper would deny that findings, whether by philosophers or students of linguistics, concerning what differences do or do not obtain in language(s) can in themselves determine the importance or significance, especially from the moral point of view, of such differences or distinctions.

There are, Popper acknowledges, "similarities" between standards and facts, or between proposals and propositions. First, proposals and propositions can be discussed and criticized, and we can come to some decision about them. Second, "there is some kind of regulative idea about both."[65] Third, "although we have no criterion of absolute rightness, we certainly can make progress [in the realm of standards]. . . . As in the realm of facts, we can make discoveries."[66] I think all three of these similarities may turn out to be important, but they are, as Popper realizes, similarities with a difference. Popper himself has already noted one difference where the first similarity is concerned, and doubtless there are other significant respects in which critical discussion and decision differ in the realms of facts and standards. The second simi-

65. Ibid., 385.
66. Ibid., 386.

larity seems the deepest and most significant; here Popper suggests the idea of a correspondence between proposals and standards analogous to the correspondence between propositions and facts. He writes that we may say of a proposal that it does or does not correspond to certain standards we have decided to adopt, but that we may also say of a standard that it is right or wrong, good or bad, valid or invalid, and so on, and by this we may mean that the corresponding proposal should or should not be accepted. This tack seems promising, but, as Popper acknowledges, "the logical situation of the regulative ideas, of 'right', say, or 'good', is far less clear than that of correspondence to the facts."[67] The third similarity Popper notes is that we can use the idea of absolute truth as "a kind of model for the realm of standards," but he cautions us that, while we may seek for absolutely right or valid proposals, we may never find them. Even so, his claim that we can make progress and that *discoveries* are possible in the realm of standards seems vulnerable to the charge of misplaced or unwarranted optimism. Popper gives these examples of discoveries in the realm of standards: "that cruelty is always 'bad'; that it should always be avoided where possible; that the golden rule is a good standard which can perhaps even be improved by doing unto others, whenever possible, as *they* want to be done by."[68] (I think Kant would have endorsed this "improvement," to the extent of recognizing that what other people want to be done unto them should be taken into account in our thinking about how they should be treated, although he, and presumably Popper also, would deny that people should always be treated as they want to be treated.)

67. Ibid., 385.
68. Ibid., 386.

The discovery that cruelty is "bad" and should be avoided could be regarded as a discovery of moral error, analogous in some respects to the discovery of the falsity of some physical theory by means of scientific testing; but the discovery that the golden rule is a good standard sounds rather like the discovery of truth, and Popper has consistently argued that we cannot know when we have found the truth. Alternatively, that cruelty is "bad" may be a conceptual truth about 'cruelty,' in which case it is no discovery, while the "discovery" that the golden rule is a good standard may after all be like the discovery that something is, provisionally, a good scientific theory—it has withstood certain tests, but what tests has the golden rule withstood? Until we have clearer examples, we will, I think, be unable to judge whether any "discoveries" we may make in the realm of standards significantly resemble "discoveries" in the realm of facts, or whether Popper's use of the term 'discoveries' in the realm of standards is little more than a play on words.

The dualism of facts and decisions, it will be recalled, was introduced by Popper at the end of *The Open Society and Its Enemies* in support of his claim that, although history has no meaning, we can give it a meaning. Historical facts as such have no meaning, and they can gain it only through our decisions. In the Addenda the dualism of facts and decisions was reformulated as the dualism of facts and standards, and it was argued that there is a decisive asymmetry between propositions and proposals. Decisions and standards, will, of course, be involved when we consider whether to accept or reject statements or propositions in the realm of facts, but these decisions and standards will have to do with questions of truth, whereas the decisions we make and the standards we invoke in appraising proposals in the realm of standards will have to do with questions of rightness and goodness. The ideas of truth and of rightness and goodness are "regulative ideas," but the logical status of regulative ideas in the moral realm is a good deal less clear, Popper thinks, than in the realm of facts. If we cannot have a criterion of absolute truth, still less can we have a criterion of absolute rightness or absolute goodness. We can, however, have standards of rightness and goodness, and, although Popper doesn't make this explicit, it is presumably from the point of view of such standards that we should evaluate any proposal that we give such-and-such a meaning to history.

The standards Popper has in mind are those of traditional liberalism, as these are reflected in "the open society." I don't think we need go into detail as to what these are, except to note one respect in which Popper is somewhat original. Rationalists, he maintains, have neglected the importance of tradition in their determination to judge all proposals solely on their own merits. By contrast Popper believes that some traditions are "precious things"; and he proposes a sociological and functional theory of tradition wherein traditions are regarded as social regularities: "The mere existence of these regularities is perhaps more important than their peculiar merits or demerits. They are needed as regularities, and therefore handed on as traditions, whether or not they are in other respects rational or necessary or good or beautiful or what you will."[69] Popper sees an analogy between the role of tradition in social life and the role of "myths and theories" in science, but gives his analogy a distinctively Popperian twist:

69. *Conjectures and Refutations,* 121, 130–131.

traditions in social life, like myths and theories in science, have a "double function" of creating an order or structure and giving us something upon which we can operate, "something we can criticize and change." Blueprints for social change "have no meaning in an empty social world, in a social vacuum," any more than would the proposal that we sweep away all science and start afresh. Although in his essay, "Toward a Rational Theory of Tradition," Popper does not speak of the "problem-situation" and the selectivity of organized inquiry, what he says about these things elsewhere may prove helpful in understanding this essay. In "On the Status of Science and of Metaphysics" Popper argues that while philosophical theories, unlike scientific theories, are irrefutable, they are nevertheless open to critical discussion. The critical discussion of philosophical theories requires, however, that we locate "the problem-situation" in which a philosophical theory emerged; only in "the setting of this *problem-situation*" is it possible to criticize, for example, Kant's determinism. In this setting we will ask questions such as whether Kant's determinism really follows, as Kant believed it did, from Newton's theory.[70] Inquiry in science and in society, no less than in philosophy, depends upon our locating the problem-situation although, of course, the ways in which it will be located and what it will consist of will vary. In science, myth and theory help give rise to problem-situations where we discover anomalies that existing theory cannot satisfactorily explain; in society, problem-situations may arise when tradition cannot cope with new social conditions such as industrialization. It is in these new problem-situations that the rationalist tradition

70. Ibid., 199–200.

of criticism becomes indispensable, where blind adherence to accepted tradition or accepted myth and theory would prove fatal. Criticism allows for the modification or rejection of any tradition, myth, or theory which fails to accommodate or account for new discoveries, but it is only in the context of a complex body of traditions that we can decide the fate of any particular tradition (just as in science we do not throw over all myths and theories when one myth or theory is refuted). The tradition of criticism in society and in science has also taught us the value and necessity of selectivity. In organized inquiry we must make *provisional* assumptions, as to the "truth" of certain theories or the "viability" of certain traditions; this is a necessary condition for the testing of any particular theory or tradition. The proposal that everything be put to the test all at once is for Popper unintelligible and potentially disastrous; no theory can reach the point of risking *everything* (where everything includes the fate of all currently accepted theories) without ceasing to be a theory.

At the beginning of "Toward a Rational Theory of Tradition," Popper remarks that Edmund Burke has never been "properly answered" by rationalists; but I believe that this essay constitutes an adequate answer to Burke, or at least the basis for such an answer, and also that Popper's answer would, with a few exceptions including Popper's penchant for terms like 'social engineering,' be largely acceptable to Burke, whose deference to tradition was limited, in principle at least, to those traditions he deemed rational. Since Popper is in my judgment a Burkian or conservative liberal, and since he seems to allow that (some) traditions may figure among the standards we should use in evaluating the rightness or goodness of various social policies and proposals, I find it strange to see him indicted as a kind of technocrat or social engineer more interested in the means of social change than in the ends toward which such changes should be directed, as being unable to account satisfactorily for the part that institutions and traditions may play in our selection of social policies, and as being insensitive to differences in the qualitative contents of the various institutions and traditions by means of which we may assess the adequacy or rightness of various social and political proposals.[71] But although these particular indictments seem to me erroneous, I cannot dismiss them entirely as simple mistakes or misreadings, as Popper tends to do,[72] for what is ultimately at issue here is, I think, the adequacy of any "conventionalist" account of morality and especially of Popper's emphasis upon the role of decision in the moral life. I shall return to this problem in the next section, but first, I shall discuss briefly one other respect in which Popper's treatment of criteria and standards yields results that are rather original and suggestive.

Historically, advocates of the open society have believed in one form or another of what Jefferson called "the pursuit of happiness," and often the commitment to the open society has arisen in part at least from the conviction that the open society is the best or most reliable means for the maximization of individual happiness or the happiness of the greatest number. Popper briefly discusses the maximization of happiness in the Addenda. First, he notes that there cannot be a criterion of absolute rightness and that the maximization of happiness

71. See Rush Rhees, "Social Engineering," *Without Answers* (London, 1969), 23–49; and Peter Winch, "Nature and Convention," *Ethics and Action* (London, 1972), 50–71, and "Popper and Scientific Method in the Social Sciences," *The Philosophy of Karl Popper*, II, 899–904.

72. See "Replies to My Critics," 1165–1172.

may have been intended as such a criterion; second, he claims that his own proposal that we adopt the minimization of misery is not intended as a criterion, although it is an improvement upon some of the ideas of utilitarianism; and third, he suggests that the "reduction of *avoidable* misery" (my italics) belongs to the "agenda" of public policy while the maximization of happiness should be left to one's private endeavor.[73] This distinction between public and private needs underscoring, since I suspect that someday Popper will be misconstrued, as Kant has been, as a puritanical moralist who disapproves of happiness. I think Popper should be interpreted as believing that happiness should be one of the standards (but not a criterion) by which individuals evaluate various proposals in the private sphere, while the reduction of avoidable misery should be one of the standards (but not a criterion) by which societies should evaluate various proposals in the realm of public policy. I think 'avoidable' deserves italicizing because (a) not all human misery is avoidable, (b) at least some of the misery that arises from the individual's failure to find happiness should be left in the private sector where it originated, and (c) to the extent that a society did set out to eliminate *all* misery, its policies would become increasingly difficult to distinguish from policies aimed at the maximization of happiness.

Scattered throughout *The Open Society and Its Enemies,* often in footnotes, there is evidence that Popper regards the maximization of happiness as the greatest pitfall into which advocates of the open society can tumble. Popper maintains that the principle 'maximize happiness' in contrast to the prin-

73. *The Open Society and Its Enemies,* II, 386.

ciple 'minimize suffering' "seems apt to produce a benevolent dictatorship."[74] He warns that from the moral point of view "suffering and happiness must not be treated as symmetrical; that is to say, the promotion of happiness is in any case much less urgent than the rendering of help to those who suffer, and the attempt to prevent suffering. (The latter task has little to do with 'matters of taste', the former much)."[75] I think there is nothing in Popper's remarks to rule out certain cases where suffering and happiness are symmetrical. In medicine the elimination of suffering may sometimes result in a feeling of relief so great as to be indistinguishable from a feeling of happiness, and in some cases social suffering may be so intense that virtually any minimization of this suffering could result in a certain amount of happiness. In cases where the social suffering is terribly intense and where also the "remedy" seems fairly obvious, we may well pursue exactly the same policy whether our ultimate goal is the minimization of suffering or the maximization of happiness. Also, I do not think Popper would wish to deny that because happiness is often dependent upon "matters of taste," feelings of deprivation in this area may be so intense as to constitute a kind of suffering. Rather I believe his remark about "matters of taste" is meant to suggest the presence of something arbitrary and inescapably subjective about the pursuit of happiness. (In Kantian terminology we have no determinate and sure concept of happiness as an end which we seek.) Although Popper doesn't spell this out, if there is such a subjective or arbitrary factor in happiness, then no dictatorship, however benevolent, could be assured of success in its efforts to maximize happiness.

As one of the principles of his "humanitarian and equali-

74. Ibid., I, 235.
75. Ibid.

tarian ethics," Popper proposes "the recognition that all moral urgency has its basis in the urgency of suffering and pain," and he argues that the "simple formula" 'minimize suffering' can be made "one of the fundamental principles (admittedly not the only one) of public policy."[76] The egalitarian aspect of this ethic is reflected in Popper's claim that there should be the least amount of suffering for all and that unavoidable suffering (as in hunger caused by food shortages) should be distributed as equally as possible.[77] Because he believes that, morally speaking, suffering and happiness or pain and pleasure are asymmetrical, Popper maintains that "both the greatest happiness principle of the Utilitarians and Kant's principle 'Promote other people's happiness. .' seem to me (at least in their formulations) wrong on this point which, however, is not completely decidable by rational argument."[78] Since Popper says so little about happiness, I think it would be unproductive to try to gauge the extent or seriousness of any disagreement he may have with Kant's ideas on happiness. Kant does say we have a direct duty to seek the happiness of others, but he does not to my knowledge say that this duty must be made a principle of public policy. In any case, I do not see how one could accept, as Popper does, Kant's doctrine that men are to be treated as ends and then balk altogether when confronted with Kant's claim that insofar as possible we should make the relative and personal ends of others our own.[79] It may be, of course, that Popper and Kant would disagree over what is possible in this regard; Popper's commitment to the principle 'minimize suffering' as a standard for evaluating policy pro-

76. Ibid.
77. Ibid., II, 285.
78. Ibid., I, 284.
79. See Paton, 172–173.

posals in the public sphere might have seemed too narrowly circumscribed to Kant—but then Kant did not experience the dictatorships, benevolent or otherwise, of our time.

Popper's remarks about happiness and suffering, while all too brief, serve to remind us that he is a systematic philosopher, as opposed to a piecemeal philosopher who specializes in one or more problems within a single philosophical area, or to a generalist who happens to write in several areas but without exploring the connections between these areas and without developing a unified point of view. As we have seen, Popper's treatment of the principles 'maximize happiness' and 'minimize suffering' reflects his anti-criterion bias, so that no matter which of these principles we come to prefer we cannot, Popper says in effect, justifiably use it as a criterion. It can at most serve as one among a number of standards (not ranked hierarchically, at least not by Popper) for the evaluation of various moral and political proposals. It should also be apparent by now that there exists a connection between Popper's preference for the principle 'minimize suffering' and his previous reflections in the Addenda and elsewhere on epistemology and methodology. Popper writes:

> I find there is some kind of analogy between this view of ethics and the view of scientific methodology which I have advocated in my *Logik der Forschung*. It adds to clarity in the field of ethics if we formulate our demands negatively, i.e., if we demand the elimination of suffering rather than the promotion of happiness. Similarly, it is helpful to formulate the task of scientific method as the elimination of false theories (from the various theories tentatively proffered) rather than the attainment of established truths.[80]

80. *The Open Society and Its Enemies,* I, 285.

The analogy Popper sees between his views on ethics and scientific method, in particular his point about the advantages of a negative formulation of our demands in ethics and science, contributes greatly to making Popper's philosophy a unified system. In my judgment only his insistence upon the use of the critical method in all areas of inquiry is more fundamental. While the knowledge of truth and the attainment of happiness are at least highly problematic in Popper's judgment, he does believe that we know how to detect error and suffering, and also that in science and in ethics progress (toward the truth and toward the good) is somehow possible. Of course, there is also a disanalogy here between error and suffering, although I believe it is of no great consequence: suffering is usually so obvious and so urgent that we need no special methodology to detect its presence, but in the case of erroneous or false theories we do need a special method, that of falsification or refutation. Here the negative formulation of our demands has two separate, but importantly related, aspects: first, there is the "demand," mentioned by Popper in the above quotation, that scientific method seek the elimination of false theories rather than the attainment of established truth; second, there is the demand, expressed by Popper in *The Logic of Scientific Discovery* and in *The Poverty of Historicism,* that natural and social laws be formulated negatively in terms of what cannot happen.[81] The principle "advantage" of a negative

81. See *The Logic of Scientific Discovery,* 69, where Popper writes that natural laws "might be compared to 'proscriptions' or 'prohibitions.' They do not assert that something exists or is the case; they deny it." According to Popper, it is not for nothing that a scientific law is called a law—a scientific law after all *forbids* something. Popper is asserting not merely that "every natural [and social] law can be *expressed* [my italics] by asserting that *such and such a thing cannot happen*" (*The Poverty of Historicism,* 61), but also the stronger thesis that scientific laws "can

formulation of our laws, or theories, as a means of satisfying the demand for a methodology aimed at the elimination of error is this: if a proposed law or theory is formulated negatively so that it tells us something cannot happen, all we need do in order to falsify this law or theory is to discover one instance of the actual occurrence of this phenomenon. On the other hand, if a law or theory is formulated positively, the discovery of numerous instances of the predicted phenomenon cannot, as the most ardent advocates of induction must concede, guarantee the truth of the law or theory in question. (I shall have more to say later about the differences between negative and positive predictions.)

While the detection of suffering, unlike the detection of error, requires no special methodology, there is, I think, a significant analogy between Popper's views on ethics and science where the *testing* of policies and proposals aimed at minimizing suffering is concerned. In social policy no less than in science we should whenever possible seek for a crucial experiment or its equivalent; here Popper's talk about social engineering and his deference, however qualified, to a unity of method in the social and natural sciences has some real bite to it, although, of course, it should be remembered that the facts discovered in social experiments cannot by themselves determine our moral decision as to the worth of the policy or proposal in question. As we have seen, Popper also believes that decision enters into our acceptance of propositions and scientific theories. I shall have more to say later about the testing of

---

never do more than *exclude certain possibilities*" (ibid., 139). For the benefit of those who doubt the existence of social laws or hypotheses, Popper in *The Poverty of Historicism,* 62, gives a number of examples, all formulated negatively.

scientific theories against what Popper calls "basic statements," but here it can be noted that two "decisions" appear to be involved, one concerning the truth of the basic statements in question and the other concerning whether to retain or abandon the theory we have tested against these basic statements. Popper emphatically argues that the decisional element in science does not warrant any conventionalist philosophy of science. However, since decisions about the fate of theories do not follow automatically from decisions about the truth of basic statements—there is usually for Popper an important middle ground between the arbitrary and the automatic—we can say that the insufficiency of basic statements to determine fully our decisions concerning whether to retain or abandon a scientific theory has an obvious parallel in the moral sphere with the insufficiency of factual discoveries to determine fully our decisions concerning whether to adopt or reject various policies and proposals. This parallel holds, I think, regardless of the outcome of our pending discussion as to whether Popper has successfully demonstrated that conventionalism is inadequate as a philosophy of science.

One further resemblance between Popper's views on ethics and science needs to be made explicit. Popper concedes that we may, for a while at least, be able to save a scientific theory from falsification by various ad hoc additions or revisions (although, of course, there will be an attendant loss in the predictive power or scope of that theory); he recommends, however, that scientists prefer the boldest theory, that is, the theory which explains the most and which runs the most risk of falsification. This distinction between "bold" theories or hypotheses and "ad hoc" ones is crucial to Popper's conception of scientific method; and it has, I think, a direct analogy in his views on piecemeal social engineering as a way of minimizing suffering or pain. However, this claim may initially seem paradoxical, since the very term 'piecemeal' suggests a cautious, essentially conservative approach to social problems. Popper himself speaks modestly where the relation between piecemeal social engineering and boldness is concerned: "I do not suggest that piecemeal engineering cannot be bold, or that it must be confined to 'smallish' problems."[82] But the examples he gives of realistic blueprints for social engineering seem anything but bold: "They are blueprints for single institutions, for health and unemployed insurance, for instance, or arbitration courts, or anti-depression budgeting, or educational reform. If they go wrong, the damage is not very great, and a re-adjustment not very difficult. They are less risky, and for this reason less controversial."[83]

To establish an analogy between Popper's preference for bold hypotheses in science and his views on piecemeal social engineering we must distinguish between two kinds of "boldness": there are bold scientific hypotheses and bold social policies which run the risk of being found, in their respective ways, deficient; and there are bold social policies and proposals—or bold social "experiments"—which, should they fail, run the risk of causing great human suffering or pain. Where the first kind of boldness is concerned, what is wrong with holistic or Utopian social engineering is that when it comes to actually testing its social policies it risks very little because, like the ad hoc improviser in science, the holistic or Utopian social planner is always willing to alter the parameters or conditions

82. *The Open Society and Its Enemies,* I, 285.
83. Ibid., 159.

of his "experiment" whenever this "experiment" encounters difficulties. If "socialized medicine" (this is my example, not Popper's) gets into difficulty, the holistic social planner may try to change the standards for what constitutes good medical care, paramedics may be substituted for doctors, and so on. As Popper's remarks in *The Poverty of Historicism* suggest, if the policies of the holistic social planner fail to make us happy, the holistic social planner may seek to suppress evidence of their failure—the bigger the project the greater this temptation will be—and he may try to accommodate *us* to his plans by altering our system of wants and expectations. In either case it will become increasingly difficult to determine what the effects of his policies actually are or how these policies might be improved.[84] Such a concern over the fate of one's pet policies is likely to involve a willingness to accept great risks where possible human dislocations and sufferings are concerned. By contrast the piecemeal social engineer is willing to take great risks where the possible discovery of weaknesses and miscalculations in his pet policies is concerned, not because he is a paragon of virtue (although Popper does tend at times to speak of him this way) but because he is committed to the method of trial and error, which means that he will be on the lookout for mistakes and for ways to learn from them. His boldness in this respect will be accompanied by a refusal to take undue risks involving possible human suffering as a result of his policies. There *is*, I think, a moral difference between the piecemeal social engineer and the holistic social planner on this point, but this difference also reflects the fact that the

84. *The Poverty of Historicism*, 83–93.

piecemeal social engineer, while he is determined to minimize human suffering, knows in advance that he is likely to make some mistakes and hopes to learn from them when he does. I cannot find a passage where Popper explicitly states that the piecemeal social engineer, like Popper's ideal scientist, will take great care to tell us in advance exactly what will count as evidence against the success of his policy, but this is surely in the spirit of what Popper does actually say. In concluding this section, I must add that it is part of the false glamour which helps make politics so dangerous that boldness is too often equated with the willingness to risk suffering, for oneself or for others, rather than with the willingness to be found in error.

I have previously quoted from the passage in *The Open Society and Its Enemies* in which Popper distinguishes between nature and convention, but now I should like to quote from it more fully so that we can evaluate Popper's claim that conventionalism in ethics, unlike conventionalism in science, need not imply arbitrariness.

The statement that norms are man-made (man-made not in the sense that they were consciously designed, but in the sense that men can judge and alter them—that is to say, in the sense that the responsibility for them is entirely ours) has often been misunderstood. Nearly all misunderstandings can be traced back to one fundamental misapprehension, namely, to the belief that 'convention' implies 'arbitrariness'; that if we are free to choose any system of norms we like, then one system is just as good as any other. It must, of course, be admitted that the view that norms are conventional or artificial indicates that there will be a certain element of arbitrariness involved, i.e., that there may be different systems of norms between which there is not much to choose. . . . But artificiality by no means implies full arbitrariness.[85]

Popper goes on to note that mathematical calculi, symphonies, and plays are highly artificial but that this does not imply that one calculus or symphony or play is as good as any other. He adds, however, that the comparison of morals with music or mathematics does not reach very far: "There is, more especially, a great difference between moral decisions and decisions in the field of art. Many moral decisions involve the life and death of other men. Decisions in the field of art are much less urgent and important. . . . Our comparison is only intended to show that the view that moral decisions rest with us does not imply that they are entirely arbitrary."[86]

It is important for us to determine what Popper's defense against allegations of arbitrariness achieves and what it fails to accomplish. I believe that his distinction between 'man-made' in the sense of being consciously designed and 'man-made' in the sense of being alterable by man helps considerably to rescue Popper from any criticism that pictures him as a super-rationalist unaware of, or indifferent toward, the role of tradition in shaping and preserving the norms we live by, while at the same time this distinction permits him to insist upon the need for critical evaluations of the adequacy of traditional norms in new problem-situations. Certainly this distinction should be kept in mind when we consider Winch's objection to Popper that "*decision* is not the fundamental concept in morality." Winch maintains that "a decision can only be made within the context of a meaningful way of life

85. *The Open Society and Its Enemies,* I, 64–65.
86. Ibid., 65.

and a moral decision can only be made within the context of a morality. A morality cannot be *based* on decisions. What decisions are and are not possible will depend on the morality within which the issues arise; and not *any* issue can arise in a given morality."[87] I think that for Popper decision is the fundamental concept in morality, although this does not imply that decision exhausts all the possibilities in the moral life; and I am in basic agreement with Popper on this issue. Morality does not consist entirely in a never-ending series of decisions or choices; we may after all become habituated, as Aristotle would say, to virtuous conduct. But even for the virtuous man new problem-situations in the moral sphere will call for decisions, sometimes momentous ones, on his part. Of course, decisions when they are made may reflect or adhere closely to the norms and traditions which prevail in a given culture; but I think Popper would be disturbed, and rightly so, by Winch's insistence that "a moral decision can only be made within the context of a morality," that "a morality cannot be *based* on decisions," and that "a given morality" determines what decisions are and are not possible. The argument developed by Winch cannot fail to remind us of what Popper has said concerning the Myth of the Framework: since the framework, a morality, determines the range of possible moral decisions and since the framework itself is not an object of possible rejection or decision, at least not of a moral decision, we appear to be stuck with, and within, the framework or morality which is "given" to us by tradition or society. If this is so, then it is Winch and not Popper who cannot make transcultural comparisons or decisions as to which of two different frameworks,

87. Winch, "Nature and Convention," 54–55.

moralities, or sets of traditions is morally preferable. To be sure, there is some truth in what Winch has said: a moral decision can, I think, only be made in a moral context, does require, in other words, the presence of other moral decisions, of norms and standards; but this need be only a way of saying that isolated, atomic judgments about right and wrong could make no sense for the same sort of reason that isolated, atomic judgments about matters of fact could make no sense. While this implies that a moral decision makes essential appeal to other moral decisions and norms, it does not limit this appeal to a single or specific morality as Winch seems to think.

The difference between "morality" and "a morality" is crucial here. It is, of course, true that anything so complex as "a morality" or body of moral norms and judgments cannot be based solely on decisions where 'decisions' refers, rather narrowly, to conscious choices made by particular individuals with no support from or ties with community or tradition. But this only shows that, morally speaking, there is no state of nature, and it clearly does not imply that we cannot choose or rationally criticize a norm, or even a complex set of norms, in the light of new problem-situations. (Similarly the fact that science is not the work of a single individual does not show that some particular scientific theory or even a complex of such theories cannot be the object of decision, acceptance or rejection, in the light of new experimental findings. Morality and science are, "by definition" if you like, both communal activities, but this does not necessarily restrict the range of choices open to members of such communities.) It may be true that certain decisions cannot be made so long as certain norms or standards are accepted and that certain problem-situations cannot even be recognized as problematic so long as certain assumptions are made, although this tells us nothing about the impossibility of rejecting or revising the norms or standards in question. It may also be true, as Winch maintains, that for any code to count as a morality it must have certain features, and he wisely invites us to consider whether, for example, we would regard something as a morality if no provision were made in this "morality" for integrity. (But integrity in a bad morality may, of course, be more reprehensible than "no integrity at all"—in this sense "bad Nazis" might be infinitely preferable from the moral point of view to "good Nazis," Nazis who exhibited integrity in their commitment to the Nazi morality.) I think there is nothing in those features which are common, or "natural," to all moralities to break the back of Popper's distinction between nature and convention, or to persuade us that, logically speaking, we cannot in extreme, and undoubtedly rare and painful, cases choose or decide to reject a particular morality without thereby deciding to give up morality altogether. Often these decisions are like the decisions described by Popper to give up some particular scientific theory or framework—we usually do so only when we believe a better alternative theory or framework is at hand.

I think that while Popper's conventionalist account of ethics can be defended against criticisms such as those advanced by Winch, his conventionalism remains deficient in several respects. It is, of course, true, as Popper points out, that if we are free to choose any system of norms we like, it does not follow that one system is just as good as any other, but here, as in the previous case of historical interpretations, Popper ultimately fails to provide us with an adequate, rational basis for preferring one system to another or to provide us with a rational demonstration that his preferred system of norms is superior to other systems of norms. Of course, a "conventional" or "artificial" account of norms will have no difficulty in dealing with "different systems between which there is not much to choose." For example, welfare state capitalism and a decentralized democratic socialism might be judged equally acceptable as alternative ways of realizing social justice, and thus from the point of view of social justice one might be rationally indifferent as to which of these systems prevails. It may also be acknowledged that "artificiality by no means implies full arbitrariness"—there may be, as Winch and others have pointed out, conceptual or other limitations upon what will count as a moral system or a morality. But the problem any conventionalist must wrestle with is how to choose rationally where there are different moral systems between which there *is* much to choose and where the question, for example, is not whether the different systems all satisfy the requirement of containing *some* provision for integrity but what sort of integrity and what norms are preferable. At this crucial point, Popper's argument trails off into analogies with music and art, although he concedes that there is "a great difference between moral decisions and decisions in the field of art." Moral decisions are more urgent, more life-and-death affairs. In fact, however, Popper's conception of decisions in ethics and in aesthetics shows a striking resemblance; in both fields his favorite metaphor of "lifting ourselves by our own bootlaces" can be seen as apropos and consistent with his desire to do justice to both "artificiality" and "objectivity." There is no natural or factual basis or justification for our choice of norms, standards, or conventions, but these may nevertheless be "'objective" and as such may admit of improvement. As Popper writes of aesthetic standards:

These standards are objective in more than one sense. They are shared, and they can be criticized. They can change (and far be it from me to say that they should not). But alterations should not be arbitrary, and even less should they be hostile to those great old standards by which we once grew, and outgrew ourselves. It is, after all, these "old standards" which represent art, and by which art must be judged at any moment in its development; and an artist who hates all the old standards is hardly an artist: what he hates is art.[88]

While this passage constitutes an eloquent and wise defense against demands for total freedom and complete novelty in the field of art, it manages, like all similar passages in Popper, to sidestep the basic issue of how we are to choose rationally between conflicting standards and how to know whether, in any given case or in general, we have succeeded in pulling ourselves up by our own bootlaces. In ethics and art, unlike in science, there is probably no common intuition that these disciplines are, or should be, regarded as "progressive," as moving somehow nearer to the truth or to the good. On the other hand, not all "old" standards in art, much less in ethics, can be regarded with equal favor, or as favorably as this passage would seem to suggest, and while conservatism in artistic and moral standards may be one way of avoiding too freakish deviations, it may not be the optimal method for progressive development. Of course, the fact that such standards may be "shared" and that they "can be criticized" might

88. "Replies to My Critics," 1176.

be helpful in certain cases; but in those cases where standards are *not* shared, a rational basis for criticism and for preferring one standard to another would seem necessary. If we cannot have criteria, then we must have standards; and when standards conflict with one another, as they sometimes do, then we need a standard for judging standards, which, according to the relativist, is just the thing we can never have. Popper's reply to the relativist is that the critical method is, or should be, something that pervades all inquiry regardless of subject matter; but he concedes that "regulative ideas" such as "good" and "right" are in crucial respects more problematic than "truth," and he seems to recognize that the chances of agreement rationally arrived at are more remote in ethics than in science. Until we learn more about exactly how "the critical method" is to work when we must choose our moral standards, it is difficult to decide whether to be more impressed by the unity of method, in this case the unity of the critical method, or by differences in subject matter, in this case the differences between morality and science. But by now this is a familiar problem where Popper exegesis and criticism are concerned.

Popper at times describes his dualism of facts and standards as a dualism of facts and decisions, but, as we have seen, he does not intend by this to deny that decision has any part in our accepting or rejecting propositions about matters of fact. He does, however, want to show that the part played by decision in science is more circumscribed than it is in the moral sphere: in deciding what ethical standards to adopt we may be said to create these standards, whereas in deciding as to the truth or falsity of scientific hypotheses or theories about matters of fact we do not (or do not "in the same sense") create the corresponding fact. Another way of putting this is that while decision enters into "the critical method" whether this method is used in the moral or in the scientific sphere, it enters in different ways and with different results. One thing that the role of decision in science does not warrant, according to Popper, is the acceptance of any form of conventionalism as a philosophy of science:

It would . . . be a complete misunderstanding to assimilate my view to any form of "conventionalism": the "conventional" or "decisional" element in our acceptance or rejection of a proposition involves in general no element of arbitrariness at all. Our experiences are not only motives for accepting or rejecting an observational statement, but they may even be described as *inconclusive reasons.* They are reasons because of the generally reliable character of our observations; they are inconclusive because of our fallibility. Decisions which are somewhat arbitrary come in only when we have to make up our minds on whether our tests are, for the time being, satisfactory, and may be concluded; or whether we are to try another test. And even these somewhat arbitrary decisions are, if considered more closely, more conjectures than decisions—conjectures, that is, that further tests will not lead to any deviating results.[89]

89. "Replies to My Critics," 1114. Popper goes on to reject Joseph Agassi's suggestion that, largely because Popper has emphasized that science is a social institution, he should recognize that his philosophy of science is after all closer to a "modified conventionalism" than to a "modified essentialism." Evidently because his recent "three worlds" metaphysics commits him to the thesis that the third world (the world of ideas) "exists" and is "autonomous," Popper now is inclined to see certain affinities between his version of realism and traditional "essentialism." It remains unclear, however, exactly how this will, or should, affect his criticism in *The Open Society and Its Enemies* and elsewhere of that "essentialism" which ranges from Aristotle and Hegel to Wittgenstein (or so Popper alleges) and which, according to Popper, has

Without spending time on the exegesis of this passage, which is a clear, general summary of Popper's position, I want to indicate briefly some of the critical difficulties confronting that position. Despite Popper's consistent opposition to conventionalism as a philosophy of science, the question of whether he has succeeded in disassociating his philosophy of science from conventionalism persists. One reason for this continuing doubt has been what Popper calls his "radical revision" of empiricism and his insistence that observations are both theory-laden and fallible: once empiricism is radically revised along Popperian lines, the problem of how to account for the "generally reliable" character of our observations without lapsing into conventionalism becomes acute. Even if it is true that our acceptance or rejection of a proposition "involves in general no element of arbitrariness at all," can Popper prove that this is so, and can he provide, if not criteria, then standards or guidelines for distinguishing an arbitrary decision to accept a proposition from a nonarbitrary one? Has he not given, even in terms of his own system, an overly simple account of the role of decision in science? And does he really help his argument by suggesting that the "somewhat arbitrary" decisions about when to conclude our tests are, more properly speaking, conjectures?

---

been the bane of Western philosophy. (Popper repeats this charge without any modification in "Replies to My Critics.") As if this were not troublesome enough, Popper goes on to add that he never fully accepted the Greek distinction between "nature" and "convention" and that while social institutions (such as science) are "man-made" and "we are therefore greatly responsible for them" they "have a certain degree of autonomy: they belong to world 3." Ibid., 1116. Popper does not consider how this membership in world 3, whereby social institutions acquire some ontological status, might affect either his methodological individualism or his political philosophy.

In *The Logic of Scientific Discovery,* which to judge from his "Replies" he still regards as a fully adequate defense against allegations of conventionalism and arbitrariness, Popper maintains that "it is *decisions* which settle the fate of theories." However, this is what the conventionalist would say and, moreover, Popper agrees with the conventionalist that our choice or selection of a theory is partially determined by "considerations of utility."[90] The basic difference between the conventionalist and Popper lies, according to Popper, in this: the conventionalist's acceptance of a theory or universal statement is governed by the principle of simplicity—"he selects that system which is the simplest"—whereas for Popper the "first thing" to be taken into account is the severity of the tests a theory has been subjected to. While Popper's conception of the severity of tests is closely linked with simplicity, simplicity for him concerns the degree of falsifiability of a hypothesis, and thus is not an aesthetic or pragmatic concept. Popper writes:

> And I hold that what ultimately decides the fate of a theory is the result of a test, i.e., an agreement about basic statements. With the conventionalist I hold that the choice of any particular theory is an act, a practical act. But for me the choice is decisively influenced by the application of the theory and the acceptance of the basic statements in connection with this application; whereas for the conventionalist, aesthetic motives are decisive.
>
> Thus I differ from the conventionalist in holding that the statements decided by agreement are *not universal but singular.* And I differ from the positivist in holding that basic statements are not justifiable by our immediate experiences, but are, from the logical point of view, accepted by an act, by a free decision. . . .

90. *The Logic of Scientific Discovery,* 108.

This most important distinction, between a justification and a *decision*—a decision reached in accordance with a procedure governed by rules—might be clarified, perhaps, with the help of an analogy: the old procedure of trial by jury.[91]

Popper proceeds to develop his analogy between the scientist's decision to accept basic statements and the verdicts of juries: juries deliberate and consider the evidence with care, according to the rules of evidence, but the verdict of the jury is a decision and not a justification in that it is not logically derivable from any other statements or from any experiences.[92] In this way Popper seeks to navigate the difficult passage between the empiricist justification of basic statements by appeals to immediate experience or to statements about such experiences and the conventionalist account of how we choose, arbitrarily and with only considerations of simplicity or of utility to assist us, our scientific theories or universal statements. Of course, we all recognize, or should, that any "act" or "free decision," whether it be in science or in law, may result in error, and that there is simply no recipe or method which guarantees its elimination; also, it may be useful, following a lead which is implicit in Popper's argument, to distinguish errors resulting from arbitrariness from errors that occur despite our best, deliberative efforts to prevent them. However, there may be cases where deliberation according to the rules of evidence would nevertheless contain an element of arbitrariness, resulting perhaps from subjective bias or even from an arbitrariness in the rules themselves. Deliberation in accordance with rules of evidence may help to minimize or even to neutralize arbitrariness, but then it may not; perhaps

91. Ibid., 109.
92. Ibid., 109–111. See also "Replies to My Critics," 1111.

we should say that deliberation in accordance with some rules is a necessary but not a sufficient condition for the avoidance of arbitrariness. What all this suggests is that while deliberation in accordance with rules may be the best we can do in a situation where there are no incorrigible "givens" and no automatic decision procedures, Popper's jury analogy is at most an answer to the charge that "free decision" in science is on his account totally or wholly arbitrary.

A more serious difficulty emerges from Popper's account of where decision or agreement enters into the scientist's activity. Popper maintains that he differs from the conventionalist "in holding that the statements decided by agreement are not *universal* but singular," and he writes, "I hold that what characterizes the empirical method is just this: that the convention or decision does not immediately determine our acceptance of *universal* statements but that, on the contrary, it enters into our acceptance of the singular statements—that is, the basic statements."[93] Popper and the conventionalist would presumably agree that the decision to accept singular or basic statements cannot, "immediately" or completely, determine our acceptance of universal statements, and both would agree further that universal statements are not verifiable. The conventionalist, however, would maintain that if decision or convention enters into our acceptance or rejection of basic statements, then it must also enter into the acceptance or rejection of universal statements when they are tested against basic statements. If the reason for insisting that decision or convention enters into our acceptance or rejection of basic statements is that the language of experience and observation is theory-

93. *The Logic of Scientific Discovery,* 108–109.

impregnated and that observation is not an infallible basis for the testing of theories, then the same reason would justify a conventionalist's insisting that decision or convention enters into the acceptance or rejection of universal statements. Since, according to Popper, basic statements must be "testable, intersubjectively, by 'observation' "[94] and since universal statements must be tested against basic statements, our acceptance or rejection of universal statements will necessarily reflect the problematic status of observation and the role of decision or convention in the determination of what is to count as an observation. Also, whether we speak of the decision or the conjecture that our testing has been sufficient, the fallibility of observation must, or should, be reflected in any claims we might make about what "severity of testing" and "crucial experiments" can actually accomplish.

Conventionalists want, I think, to say two things about the theories of science: first, that such theories can be preserved indefinitely from falsification so long as we are willing to tack on ad hoc hypotheses or to modify the definitions within our theories; and second, that because of the complexity of scientific theories and the large number of auxiliary hypotheses or assumptions used in the testing of such theories, we can never be certain when a theory has been refuted or falsified or whether, in the event a theory appears to have been refuted, the fault lies in the theory or in the auxiliary hypotheses we have used in testing the theory. In response to the first point Popper concedes that the theories of science can be preserved, if not indefinitely then for some time, by the addition of ad hoc hypotheses, although such hypotheses may themselves

94. Ibid., 102.

turn out to be falsifiable (the classic example of this, which Popper cites, was the postulation of an outer planet to explain the motions of Uranus, which seemed to falsify Newton's theory); in any event, a theory that can be preserved from falsification by the addition of ad hoc hypotheses now becomes a new or different theory and, as such, subject to new tests aimed at its falsification. In *The Logic of Scientific Discovery* Popper writes, "as regards *auxiliary hypotheses* we decide to lay down the rule that only those are acceptable whose introduction does not diminish the degree of falsifiability or testability of the system in question, but, on the contrary, increases it."[95] According to the conventionalist, another possible way of saving a theory from falsification is by modifying the definitions within the theory. Popper would permit changes in the explicit definitions of a theory if such changes prove "useful" and provided they are regarded as modifications of the theory; he would also allow the elimination of "undefined universal names" (such as 'energy') or changes, provided they are not done surreptitiously, in the usage of "undefined concepts" (such as 'movement' or 'mass-point').[96]

Ultimately Popper acknowledges quite candidly that the only way to avoid conventionalism is to make the *decision* to avoid all conventionalist strategies. Conventionalism, according to Popper, is a coherent and defensible, though finally unacceptable, philosophy of science; it deserves much credit for clarifying in an anti-inductivist way the relation between

95. Ibid., 82–83. See also Popper's "Autobiography," 32–33. For some objections to Popper's efforts to tie degrees of testability to degrees of content in this way, see Adolf Grünbaum, "Can a Theory Answer More Questions than One of its Rivals?," *British Journal for the Philosophy of Science,* 27 (1976), 1–23.

96. *The Logic of Scientific Discovery,* 83–84.

theory and experiment and for recognizing the importance of "our actions and operations, planned in accordance with conventions and deductive reasoning."[97] Speaking generally, I believe that Popper's philosophy of science can be regarded as an attempt not to refute conventionalism (no philosophy can be refuted, Popper believes, although certainly many philosophies are false), but rather to relocate and redescribe, often in a more complex way, the role of decision in science to which conventionalists have, Popper believes, attached an exaggerated and misleading significance.

Popper's general or overall answer to the second point made by the conventionalist (that owing to the complexity of the universal statements and theories of science as well as to the large number of auxiliary hypotheses or assumptions used in the testing of scientific theories, we can never be certain as to when or in what respects a theory has been falsified) would be as follows. First, Popper would agree that we cannot be *certain* as to when or in what respects a theory may be correctly said to be falsified; and second, he would acknowledge the systematic character of a scientific theory, but without despairing over our ability to conjecture (reasonably) as to what part of a scientific theory or system is responsible for that theory's being falsified. "Newton's theory is a system. If we falsify it, we falsify the whole system. We may perhaps put the blame on one of its laws or another. But this means only that we *conjecture* that a certain change in the system will free it from falsification; or in other words, that we conjecture that a certain alternative system will be an improvement, a better approximation to the truth."[98]

97. Ibid., 80.
98. "Replies to My Critics," 982.

The arguments Popper gives for sticking to his falsifiability criterion as a way of demarcating science (from metaphysics, mathematics, and logic) are numerous and intricate, but they seem to turn on one argument from common sense, one argument about what is typical of scientific theories, and a logical argument from what is or is not required for falsification.[99] What I have called the argument from common sense is directed against Pierre Duhem's criticism of "crucial experiments," which shows, according to Popper, only that crucial experiments cannot prove that a theory is true, not that they cannot refute a theory: "Admittedly Duhem is right when he says that we can test only huge and complex theoretical systems rather than isolated hypotheses; but if we test two such systems which differ in one hypothesis only, and if we can design experiments which refute the first system while leaving the second very well corroborated, then we may be on *reasonably safe ground* if we attribute the failure of the first system to that hypothesis in which it differs from the other."[100]

99. Someone might wonder how Popper can propose falsifiability as a criterion for demarcating science from nonscience, given his disdain for what he calls criterion philosophies in the Addenda to *The Open Society and Its Enemies.* Popper's rejection of the possibility of a general criterion of truth can easily be squared with his proposal of falsifiability as a criterion of demarcation; in the case of his proposed criterion we have a *method* or way of deciding when a theoretical system is conventional or empirical (and this method, Popper insists, does not concern the logical form of the system or the meaning of the concepts it contains). See *The Logic of Scientific Discovery,* 81–82, and Popper's "Autobiography," 32, where he concedes, however, that "logically speaking falsifiability, or testability, cannot be regarded as a very sharp criterion."

100. *The Poverty of Historicism,* 132, my italics. In *The Open Society and Its Enemies,* II, 364, Popper writes, "But Duhem wrote before Einstein, and before Eddington's crucial eclipse observation; he even wrote before the experiments of Lummer and Pringsheim which, by falsifying the formulae of Rayleigh and Jeans, led to the Quantum theory."

I have italicized 'reasonably safe ground' as a way of calling attention to the tentative nature of the decision that the failure of the first system is due to the hypothesis in which it differs from the second, and I have characterized Popper's argument in this passage as a common-sense argument because, while the conclusion arrived at in his example seems reasonable, it is judgmental in the sense of not being, strictly speaking, logically necessary or mandatory. Popper spells out the reasons why this latitude exists in a passage in *The Logic of Scientific Discovery* in which he tells us what falsification by means of *modus tollens* can and cannot show. Let p be a conclusion of a system t of statements consisting of theories and initial conditions; then by *modus tollens,* if p is derivable from t and if p is false, then t is also false. Popper writes, "By means of this mode of inference we falsify *the whole system* (the theory as well as the initial conditions) which was required for the deduction of the statement p, i.e., of the falsifying statement. Thus it cannot be asserted of any one statement of the system that it is, or is not, specifically upset by the falsification. Only if p is *independent* of some part of the system can we say that this part is not involved in the falsification."[101] Popper then goes on to illustrate this by discussing how different levels of universality may lead us to think of some definite hypothesis as false. Imagine that a well-corroborated, older hypothesis or system is deductively explained by a new hypothesis of a higher level of universality, and imagine further that this new hypothesis is tested by some of its consequences which show it to be false. "Then we may well attribute the falsification to the new hypothesis alone. We shall then seek, in its stead, other high-level generalizations, but we shall not feel

101. *The Logic of Scientific Discovery,* 76.

obliged to regard the old system, of lesser generality, as having been falsified."[102] Popper's language here is cautious ("we may well") not only as a reflection of his overall fallibilism but mainly because *modus tollens* does not allow us to discriminate logically between those parts of the system which are and are not responsible for the falsity of *p;* only if *p* is independent of some part of the system can we say that this part is not involved in the falsification. In *Conjectures and Refutations,* discussing Quine's "holistic view of empirical tests," Popper writes, "It has to be admitted that we can often test only a large chunk of a theoretical system, and sometimes perhaps only the whole system, and that, in these cases, it is sheer guesswork which of its ingredients should be held responsible for any falsification; a point which I have tried to emphasize—also with reference to Duhem—for a long time past. Though this argument may turn a verificationist into a sceptic, it does not affect those who hold that all our theories are guesses anyway."[103] I suppose a verificationist or an inductivist might be tempted to reply that there is nothing here to *turn* Popper into a skeptic because anyone who believes that "all our theories are guesses anyway" is already a skeptic, and as such will scarcely be affected one way or the other by holistic accounts of scientific theories as systems. Actually, however, I think that Popper in much, though not all, of what he says about theories as being guesses, is mainly reminding us of the merits of fallibilism; here the fact that *modus tollens* cannot inform us as to which hypothesis in a system is responsible for that system's being false shows us how misplaced certainty is in affairs of science, but for Popper this is no reason to despair.

102. Ibid., 77. Popper describes this advance to theories of an ever-higher generality as a "quasi-inductive evolution" (ibid., 276–278).
103. *Conjectures and Refutations,* 239.

The acceptance of "traditional" or "background" knowledge is known by the falsificationist to be a tentative and risky business: "every bit of it is open to criticism, even though only in a piecemeal way. We can never be certain that we shall challenge the right bit; but since our quest is not for certainty, this does not matter."[104] Clearly Popper did not intend to take certainty away from verificationists and inductivists only to give it to falsificationists; however, there may still be good, informed guesses (as in Popper's own example of different levels of universality) as to what part of a system is responsible for that system's being false. This is why I believe Popper's position here can best be construed as a common-sense argument: reasons for believing some part of a system to be accountable for the falsity of that system cannot, strictly speaking, be shown to be logically conclusive, but we would be deficient in good sense if, on these grounds, we were to despair of our ability to explain or isolate what it is in any particular system that is responsible for that system's failure to withstand severe testing.

Popper's second argument against the interpretation which conventionalists place upon the holistic or systematic character of scientific theory consists of an appeal, illustrated by numerous examples, to what is typical of scientific theories. According to Popper, and I believe he is correct here, "most physical theories are pretty free of immunizing tactics and *highly falsifiable to start with.* As a rule, *they exclude an infinity of conceivable possibilities.*"[105] The reader will find the exchanges between Lakatos, Kuhn, Putnam, and Popper instructive on this point, which obviously depends upon detailed forays into both the history of scientific revolutions and the structure of

104. Ibid., 238.
105. "Replies to My Critics," 985.

scientific theories. Popper in effect divides theories in the physical and social sciences into three categories, which are evident from some of his examples: Newton's theory was falsifiable and highly so (the greater the level of universality the greater the number of potential falsifiers a theory will have); Marx's theory of revolution started out as a falsifiable and hence bona fide scientific theory but was later altered by various conventionalist strategems adopted by its defenders (Marx told us the circumstances under which revolution was not to be expected, but the Russian Revolution occurred under just those circumstances, and, therefore, Marxism as a scientific theory was falsified); psychoanalysis was always a conventionalist charade, pretending to be empirical and scientific but actually being unfalsifiable (it is notorious, Popper alleges, that psychoanalysts can explain any behavior within their theoretical framework and that no behavior can stand as evidence against their theory). Popper's discussions of these three sorts of theories are lively but especially clear,[106] and I shall pass on to his third argument.

Popper's basic contention in regard to scientific theories is that not only are they highly falsifiable to start with, but that "although we have no criterion of truth, and no means of being even quite sure of the falsity of a theory, it is easier to find out that a theory is false than to find out that it is true."[107] The conventionalist reply to this would, I think, be that even if we forgo entirely the strategem of tacking on ad hoc hypotheses as a means of preventing the falsification of a theory, we can still come no closer to finding out that a theory is false than to finding out that it is true, and the reason for this is

106. See Popper's "Autobiography," 32–33, and "Replies to My Critics," 1004–1009.

107. *Objective Knowledge,* 318.

that the testing of any scientific theory requires the use of a perhaps indefinitely large number of auxiliary hypotheses. Whether or not Popper's proposal that we use only those auxiliary hypotheses that increase the falsifiability of a theory is feasible, the fact that any auxiliary hypotheses are used is fatal to Popper's claim that it is easier to find out that a theory is false than to find out that it is true.

In this connection I wish to examine Popper's reply to Hilary Putnam's "The 'Corroboration' of Theories." Putnam had argued (1) that theories alone do not imply predictions but that auxiliary statements or statements of boundary conditions (including initial conditions) are needed for prediction, (2) that such auxiliary statements are frequently "highly risky suppositions," and (3) that because we are "very unsure" of the auxiliary conditions "we cannot regard a false prediction as definitely falsifying a theory; theories are not strongly falsifiable."[108] Popper would, I think, have no quarrel with (2) except to point out that what Putnam calls auxiliary statements may be no more risky than many other suppositions, including especially scientific theories; and the first part of (3) seems compatible with Popper's own conclusion that we can never be "quite sure of the falsity of a theory." Nevertheless, Popper would insist that scientific theories are strongly falsifiable, and one reason for this emerges from his reply to Putnam's first point, that theories alone do not imply predictions but that auxiliary statements or statements of initial conditions are needed for predictions. Popper notes that as early as *The Logic of Scientific Discovery* he had pointed out that theories alone do not imply predictions but that he had also insisted that basic statements may sometimes contradict

108. *The Philosophy of Karl Popper*, I, 228.

a theory. Putnam's fundamental error, according to Popper, can be traced to his overlooking the existence of two different kinds of prediction. While it is true that without initial conditions we can obtain no positive predictions from any theory, we can obtain negative predictions without auxiliary statements or what Popper here calls "statements of initial conditions." From the theory 'All swans are white' we obtain the prediction 'You will not encounter at 10:00 P.M. tomorrow a black swan,' this negative prediction being, according to Popper, not a basic statement but a nonexistential proposition 'There does not exist such and such a thing, at such and such a space-time region.' This negative prediction, while it is not a basic statement, can be refuted by basic statements. In other words, I can tell you what you will not encounter tomorrow, and if you do encounter it my negative prediction will have been falsified. Popper concludes that "auxiliary hypotheses" may be needed for some "sophisticated tests" of a highly informative theory, but some tests are "quite crude. If the force of gravity were to become a repulsive force Putnam would soon notice a difference."[109] The argument now turns not upon whether a scientific theory is a system or whether it is typically falsifiable; and all Popper needs to make his essential point is to show that *some* theories are falsifiable without the use of auxiliary statements. This he has accomplished in his discussion of negative predictions.

Let us suppose, as I think is true, that induction, though as yet unjustified, is justifiable. If true, this would, of course, require us to redraw Popper's proposed line of demarcation between science and nonscience: scientific hypotheses would

109. "Replies to My Critics," 997–998.

now have to be considered falsifiable *and* genuinely confirmable. The problem of demarcation, as Popper acknowledges, involves an ultimate decision, but it seems to me counterintuitive to say that scientific and empirical hypotheses are falsifiable but not confirmable. Should we draw the line as I have suggested, we can still exclude the pseudoscientific. If, as Popper alleges, psychoanalysis (or any theory) is formulated in such a way that it can only be confirmed and never falsified, then it is simply not a scientific theory and will fall on the wrong side of our demarcation line.

Imagine, however, that the philosophically worst comes to pass. Falsification and induction both are judged to present insoluble difficulties; Putnam's judgment that the quest for demarcation lines between the scientific and the nonscientific is old hat comes to prevail; and in the philosophy of science we are left with some version of conventionalism. I think it not unreasonable to imagine that Popper's basic insights into the differences between the scientific and the pseudoscientific, and into the differences between science and morality, would, like the phoenix of myth and cliché, rise from the ashes and take new form. Conventionalists would, I think, become tempted to distinguish between the conventionality of scientific decision and the conventionality of moral decision and to note differences between the conventionalist strategems used in answering questions of fact and those used in answering the question whether history has any moral meaning or significance. I hope that one of Popper's insights *will* prevail, namely, that there is a sense, and a very important one, in which the question whether history has meaning is a self-referential question, or in other words a question about what meaning *we* decide or choose to give to history.

Index